Shaolin Kempo Unveiled

Shaolin Kempo Unveiled

Presented by:

Master Marlon Wilson
&
Professor Tom Ingargiola

Copyright © 2019 by Marlon Wilson & Tom Ingargiola.
Cover Design by Mike Hennessey

ISBN:	Softcover	978-1-7960-6875-7
	eBook	978-1-7960-6881-8

All rights reserved. No part of this book may be reproduced or transmitted in any form or by any means, electronic or mechanical, including photocopying, recording, or by any information storage and retrieval system, without permission in writing from the copyright owner.

Any people depicted in stock imagery provided by Getty Images are models, and such images are being used for illustrative purposes only.
Certain stock imagery © Getty Images.

Print information available on the last page.

Rev. date: 11/05/2019

To order additional copies of this book, contact:
Xlibris
1-888-795-4274
www.Xlibris.com
Orders@Xlibris.com
805018

CONTENTS

Preface ix
About The Authors xiii
Introduction xv

Shaolin Kempo Karate 1
Precepts for Training and Development As a Warrior 13
The Five Animals of Shaolin Kempo 17
The Basics 22
Tool Kit of Strikes 32
Shaolin Kempo Weaponry Training 47
Strategy & Tactics 49
Fighting Tactics 55
The Master Keys 62

Recommended Readings 77
Appendix 1: From White Belt to Black Belt 79
Appendix 2: Sample Questions For Grading 91

Disclaimer: Please note that the publisher and authors of this instructional book are NOT RESPONSIBLE in any manner whatsoever for any injury or legal action that may result from practicing the techniques and / or following the instructions given that martial arts training can be dangerous, both to yourself and others, even when practiced with caution. You should always consult with and train with qualified martial arts instructors. The use of the martial moves/theories and strategies in our book may lead to legal issues depending on the laws of the land. We strongly suggest that each reader inform themselves of the laws governing self defense and the use of force wherever they are and govern themselves accordingly. As the physical activities described herein may be too strenuous in nature for some readers, it is also recommended that a physician be consulted prior to training.

Additionally, it should be noted that the views of the authors are their own personal views. They do not necessarily represent the views of any Federal, State or local entities or corporations.

Preface

Shaolin Kempo is a dynamic martial art form that has wide spread branches throughout North America and Europe, yet it has been largely misunderstood and misrepresented for a variety of factors. This book is a collaborative work on the part of two Shaolin Kempo Masters from two different countries and two divergent backgrounds. The goal of Shaolin Kempo Unveiled is to demystify the art of Shaolin Kempo and assist its multitude of practitioners to arrive at a better understanding of its foundation, its core and its goals. The authors will introduce the master keys to unlock the tremendous power and effectiveness unexplored by many Shaolin Kempo students. Follow the teachings in this book and not only will you grow as a martial artist, the effectiveness of your self-protection skills will increase exponentially. This book is not intended to be an end product in and of itself. It is intended to be a starting platform to unite and promote a better understanding and practice of the venerable art of Shaolin Kempo.

As authors, we have chosen the term Shaolin Kempo because this is the term that is most widely used to depict and to describe our chosen art form. However, we could have easily used the term Kempo or Shaolin Kempo Karate. The official name, Shaolin Kempo Karate is the most true way to represent the name of our chosen style. However, the more widely used name, "Shaolin Kempo" has been used throughout this work.

We welcome everyone to test these concepts and challenge anything that is presented in our book. However, be willing to train it out first. Training is truth, so truly wrestle with it and work it out, before altering it or dismissing it.

The fact that the two of us can maintain a master-student relationship, but also, express the differences in our approach and expression of this art represents a powerful testimony of the adaptability and integrity of the pursuit and study of Shaolin Kempo.

~ An Invitation ~

My name is Steven Castelli and I am the Chief Instructor of Shaolin Self Defense Centers of Babylon, New York. I have been studying under the tutelage of Professor Ingargiola for over three decades. Over the years, my relationships with Tom have ranged from my sensei, training partner, cornerman, business partner, and mentor. However, I have always considered him a friend and confidant.

The movements and techniques he taught me as a toddler are the same ones I still train with and teach at my school today. When I read this book, it reminds me of the many past lessons and experiences I have experienced under my Kempo training with "Professor I". As you read this fantastic training guide I hope you realize that the ideas, concepts and techniques are the same ones that I have had the privilege of experiencing first hand for over thirty years.

Please remember that as you progress in your training, you would be wise to re-read the book more than once. As you progress, so will your understanding and interpretations of the material presented throughout this training guide. Please remember the word "Sensei" can be translated as "One who has traveled down the path further". Take the experiences and wisdom from Kempo masters who have travelled down the path further to guide/assist you in your personal journey.

Lastly, I would like to personally invite you to visit my school if you find yourself in New York to train for a few days. I know that many of you reading this guide could be from varied locations throughout the United States and most likely from other countries as well. To experience firsthand, the insight and knowledge highlighted by this training guide would be of

great benefit to you in your Kempo journey. I am about one hour east of New York City, so if you find yourself on a vacation or business trip in the NY City area, I do hope that you seize the opportunity and contact me to make arrangements. Additionally, if you are looking to contact Master Wilson or Prof. Ingargiola please reach out to me and I will forward your inquiry.

Respectfully,

Master Steven P. Castelli, 7 Degree Blackbelt
630 Sunrise Highway, West Babylon, New York, 11704
631-321-1910 www.shaolinkempo.com info@shaolinkempo.com

About The Authors

Professor Tom Ingargiola has been studying martial arts since high school and has been teaching Shaolin Kempo since 1985 (www.shaolinkempo.com). He achieved rank in the art of Shaolin Kempo under several notable instructors. He fought professionally and retired as the New York State Super-Welterweight Kickboxing Champion (www.uskba.com). He was promoted to Professor (10th Degree) status in 2006 by Professor Feliciano Ferreira of Hawaii. He has worked as a Correction Officer at Rikers Island in New York City, where he was valedictorian and classified as a pistol expert, as well. He is currently employed by a security organization in the United States. He has toured North America presenting Shaolin Kempo to various Shaolin Kempo clubs for over three decades. He has received numerous awards and commendations: Inducted into the United Martial Artist Hall of Fame in 1999; Male Competitor of the year in 2001 and in 2005 his school was named School of the Year by Action Martial Arts magazine. Additionally, he recently completed his Master's degree in Business Administration at Grantham University.

Marlon Wilson is a fifth degree master of Shaolin Kempo. He has been teaching Shaolin Kempo in Montreal, Quebec since 1998 (www.shaolinkempo.ca). He began his martial arts at the age of 15 with Judo. He achieved the rank of brown belt.

After taking some Kyokushin for a few months and Aikido for six months, he came across a Shaolin Kempo school. This was to be his first taste of his greatest martial art love. The achievement of shodan (first-degree black belt) brought him to a place that needed a deeper understanding and knowledge of the history and application of this art. He started to teach for his teachers and then later on his own. His passion for learning exploded in the richness and reward of being a teacher. He remains forever a student. The responsibility to his students fueled yet another powerful passion: The need to learn everything about Shaolin Kempo and how to train more effectively. As his training continued, his depth, knowledge and skill as a martial artist grew. When the last of the available teacher of Shaolin Kempo in his area closed their doors, there was a dilemma. In a panic and feeling pressure to take over the school along with the considerable business expenses, he typed a post on a forum entitled "losing Shaolin Kempo". Of the many responses he received, one stood out, no suggestions, no attacks just a simple request, "Why don't you call me and tell me what is happening, if you want?" The sign off said that the response came from a Shaolin Kempo master. Marlon called, and that began the journey to a whole new level of learning, studying and training in Shaolin Kempo. This master's teachings and training methods unified everything he had learned and studied from all his varied searching. This began his journey to mastery...the poster who responded was Professor Thomas Ingargiola.

Introduction

GETTING STARTED ON YOUR PATH - OLD VS NEW

A few words from Prof. Ingargiola

There are many thoughts offered by many people that the old ways of training in the martial arts are better than the more modern ways. However, there are also many people that believe the exact opposite. They view modern training methods as superior to the ways of old. A question that has been posed to me many times is, "Is ground fighting better than stand up or vice versa?" My best answer to this, and many related questions, is the same way I choose to answer most student questions. The answer is "YES!"

At first glance, you might say this is a cop-out answer or one that makes no sense. Let me explain further. I have been involved in teaching martial arts for over 3 decades, and I have purposely chosen to use the word "YES" to most questions. I have fought many martial artists in various types of matches over the years. Some matches I fought very publicly, as a paid professional fighter, and some in less public settings. All I can say is a fighter wins fights, not systems or a particular style.

Bruce Lee said it best, "Before I learned the art, a punch to me was just a punch, a kick was just a kick. After I'd learned the art, a punch was no longer a punch, a kick no longer a kick. Now that I understand the art, a punch is just a punch, a kick is just a kick" (Lee, Bruce, Tao of Jeet Kune Do, p.70, Black Belt Books, Valencia CA.). Systems, styles and training methods do not win fights, fighters do! We must all acknowledge that there are many components that make a fighter effective or ineffective.

There is knowledge, application, experience, timing, speed, strength and flexibility. There is, also confidence in one's ability. Before I started competing and traveling across the country, I believed that martial arts were 80% physical and 20% mental. Now that I understand martial arts, I have come to realize that these ratios have flipped completely. Confidence in one's ability, is the glue that brings knowledge, experience, timing, and the physical attributes together.

This book was written for the serious martial artist. I know that you are, most likely, a serious martial artist who picked this book to gain a deeper understanding and appreciation of your chosen art of Shaolin Kempo. If you were just in it for the exercise, to impress someone or yourself, to brag about being a Black belt, or just to lose weight and get in shape, you probably would not have spent the time, effort and money to acquire this book and its knowledge.

Now, there is nothing wrong with practicing martial arts for any of the above reasons. In fact, this statement brings us full circle to the title of this section, "Old vs. New." Which way is better? Is the Old way of training better? Are the modern methods more correct? Is being a stand up fighter better? Is being a ground fighter better? My answer is "YES" to all of these questions. Yes, in that in terms of self-defense, everything is situational and all decisions must be viewed in the totality of the circumstances of the moment. In Shaolin Kempo there are many legends and rumors, as well as a good amount of hearsay. Some Shaolin Kempo masters in our lineage have been credited with saying such statements as, "Class has not begun until there is blood on the floor" or perhaps you heard it this way, "Class is not over until there is blood on the floor". I was not there just as you were not, either. Whether this is a statement that was uttered by someone at some point in time makes no difference in the real scheme of things, nor to your progression in Shaolin Kempo. This is just another way of saying, "YOU GET OUT OF IT WHAT YOU PUT INTO IT". However, it just makes it more memorable. You might have heard of stories of old, where students drive their hands into buckets of varying materials or have their teachers poke at them with sticks of fire, etc., etc. I have never been one to try too hard to impress the students I teach or the people I have fought against. A fight is a fight and the goal is to get the encounter over as quickly and efficiently as possible, without getting injured.

You might think the above paragraph is an "anti-old way" of training statement. It is not. Let me now pick on some modern statements and ideas as well. I have seen some schools that actually have used these words in their marketing material, "The martial arts used to be a way to defend yourself from attacks. Now, it is a modern day fitness program that will help you lose weight and have fun in a positive environment." You have most likely heard your own various takes on similar marketing messages. All I can say is that martial arts are and always will be a way to defend yourself against attacks. The effect of losing weight and having fun are just an extra bonus, as far as I am concerned.

Likewise, I have seen some schools alter their curriculum in such a manner that it is in no longer recognizable or functional. Perhaps, these schools had the goal of student retention and they may even enjoy temporary profits. In the long run, know that water always seeks its level. By this I mean, that the truth always comes out. Schools and teachers who are true to their standards and goals and operate honorably, will stand the test of time and those that follow the current craze or trend will end up falling by the wayside. Lastly, I see many schools selling gizmos and gadgets to help students with various elements of their training. The list goes from items to help you stretch, such as racks, bands or special tonics and vitamins to special gloves or wraps that will enable you to hit harder. Blah blah blah ... the list goes on and on. Our program is better than theirs. Our school is better than theirs. We have the secrets and are willing to share them with you because, you are special...the list can go on and on.

If you have made it to Black Belt, I am quite sure you have already figured out that there are no secrets in martial arts and no short cuts! If you want to get better at sparring, you must spar under competent instructors who have demonstrated their ability to spar. If you want to get better at stretching you must stretch each day. If you want to lose weight, you must eat in moderation, eat better and exercise more. To try to learn martial arts without ever fighting is like trying to become a master painter in a dark room or trying to learn how to swim without water. To learn and master the martial arts you must "DO". IT IS THAT SIMPLE AND THAT HARD. Too many modern day instructors use class time to talk about themselves or to pitch new programs or pieces of equipment. I know that it sounds as though I am picking on modern ways of training, however, that is not true. There are many modern concepts and training tools that I completely accept. Some of the new striking bags that have been introduced over the years are fantastic. Having the ability to videotape your training sessions for extra review at the end of night is a great tool. Modern timing equipment, heart monitors and tracking devices are all tools to help one achieve goals. In the end, you are either moving in one of two directions. Closer to your goal or further away. YES! IT IS THAT SIMPLE!!

One must be true to their goal. In the dojo, in the business world, and in family life, one must always make sure that their short term ACTIONS are consistent with their long term GOALS. When this is true, good things will flourish. When it is not true, you will face obstacle after obstacle.

There are different methods, ways, tools, drills and strategies to achieve different goals in the dojo and in life. You must keep your short term actions consistent with your long term goals. If your goal is to lose pounds and unwind after work, it does not make sense for you to join the gym in your neighborhood because it touts that it is the premiere mixed martial arts school in town. Likewise, if your goal is to learn how to compete in mixed martial art competitions, you should probably not enroll in your local civic center's weekly self defense class.

You need to take control of your path. You must scout out a few schools and see what is out there and which school is most likely the best fit for where you are currently with your training and your current goals. People change over time, and schools change over time, so this is more of a process than a one-time decision. You have to make sure that you, your school, your instructors and your chosen style/method are a match. Most likely, it is going to be a school/style that utilizes both traditional and modern training methods. Things that are older tend to be time tested and have a strong foundation. However, they can and do, run their course over time. The opposite is true as well. Modern training methods can at times be superior and yield better and faster results. There are also modern methods out there that are just a fad or a new commercialized twist that does not stand the test of time. The Yin and Yang theory is the best way to wrap up the controversy of Old vs. New. For true balance, there must be yin present in the yang section and there must be yang present in the yin section. A mixture of old and new will help you achieve a more balanced training approach. Take a moment and look at the picture below to better understand what I mean.

So the question of what is better, old training methods or modern training methods is in the end, a weak question. The real question is about your current training methods and if they are assisting you in achieving your goals? If you do not know what your goals are, take a moment and reflect on it and write it down and share it with some of the higher ranking black belts in your school or system. Remember, YOUR SHORT TERM ACTIONS MUST BE CONSISTENT WITH YOUR LONG TEtRM GOALS!!!

MAKE THE EFFORT TO FIND A GOOD TEACHER

- A few words from Master Marlon Wilson

Another aspect of old vs. new rests at the heart of training. The right training and teaching comes to the student from their teacher. I drive over 14 hours several times a year to train with Prof. Ingargiola. The travel is well worth it.

The practice of martial arts in the roots of its history often encompassed a warrior ethos. The reason people trained did not mainly spring from fear. The root of training was love and personal development. The love of your nation, culture, family, beliefs, freedom and the protection of these, motivated a person to become a warrior. This meant that they were willing to enter training as though entering a forge, to become something new. This was necessary on many levels, not the least of reasons being, the protection of family and society. The "old ways" indoctrinated and educated the trainees. Masters were not brutes. They were educated scholars, poets, teachers and leaders with brutal skill sets. They had strong bonds to shared beliefs and a strict ethic of right and wrong. They had a code. Certainly, there were some who slipped by and learned without truly believing, yet there was a concerted effort to avoid such "unworthy" ones from gaining the highest levels of skill and influence. There exists many schools today that train with a quasi religious atmosphere and teach culture and philosophy as part of the art. At the other end of the spectrum, there are modern schools that are all about fear, power and self-preservation with zero regard for any idea of a concept of good, that extends beyond their small circle. They generally do not consider an ethic that comes with an allegiance to something greater than themselves.

To my thinking, a balance leads to superior attitude, superior training and superior martial artists and practitioners. A balance leads to students and teachers worthy of the title of Warrior. Shaolin Kempo descends from a warrior history, yet the considerable demands of running a school as a business and our modern world (and modern "parenting" for that matter) presents a challenge to the propagation of the warrior ethos. Some of us succeed in attaining a balance and maintaining the focus of our conscience and teachings while some others, less so. Do your research to find the right teacher for you, and investigate well any school before joining. Excellent warriors exist in every style, they have not given up their duty, do not give up on finding them.

Shaolin Kempo Karate

WHAT IS SELF DEFENSE?

Self defense, at it's highest level, completely avoids physical confrontation. Sun Tzu said in The Art of War, "The skillful leader subdues the enemy without any fighting" (Section 3.6).

We train to be able to end an unavoidable bad situation, quickly. The first principle of self defense is in awareness. Avoid places and situations where violence is likely or known to occur. This includes planning ahead, always knowing your exits and paying attention to the environment. The environment includes watching for signs of escalation. Some signs of impending escalation to violence includes a sudden change in behavior by someone in a confrontational situation. Someone shouting suddenly becoming quiet can be just as much an indication as someone going from quiet to loud. Anyone entering your "security zone" in terms of closeness to you. One or more other people moving a little closer to you while you are expressing your disagreement with another or your attention is fixed elsewhere. Being approached by a stranger in an isolated or semi-isolated situation. Awareness is your best defense! When you notice these things seek to remove yourself from the situation as quickly and as non-confrontationally as possible.

When confronted with verbal aggression, exercise your de-escalation skills. Do not just try to "talk them down". You can actively listen, empathize and re-formulate what they are saying in your own words. This let's them know that they have been heard. Take a non-confrontational stance with your hands visible and open. Apologize and offer to make amends, if possible, for whatever offense they claim you have given.

In the end, if you must use your physical skills, the training and teachings in Shaolin Kempo Unveiled will serve you well. Jennifer Budkewich, a Shaolin Kempo student living in Vienna, Austria reminded us to point out clearly here at the beginning of this book that self defense is not made primarily for young hormone- filled athletic males. Here are her own words:

Having been a girl in martial arts, I would never and will never be as strong as most of the men I worked with, so I used the master principles of the techniques to my advantage, made them work for me, my height, strength, and other capabilities. That's why I love the principle of fighting dragon style so much - for one, it combines all the animals, and also you get out of the visible line of attack, create targets by moving the opponent in the direction I want him with little force, and striking pressure points, nerves and any surface that promises maximum results with little strength. If the attacker is too tall for me to take down, kick him in the groin to make him bend over and bring his head, throat, ears, eyes and all those wonderful targets to me. No brute strength required. Joint locks and trigger punches work for everyone if you know how to use them. "Hit them where the sun doesn't shine, and then even if your opponent is drunk or on drugs and impervious to pain at the moment, the nerves and mechanics of the body will still render him at a disadvantage... Plus, the element of surprise works so well - an opponent won't guard his face as much when he doesn't believe that his opponent is worthy or capable of defending herself. That split second it takes for him to realize he's not dealing with a helpless little girl is all you need to do your damage and get out of there safely. This is true for street fights as well as martial arts training - even when we had new students in our class who saw I had a black belt tied around my waist they often underestimated what a 17 year old girl could do. Fight like a girl - I still want to make that sentence into a daunting threat instead of an insult. - **Jennifer Budkewitsch, Nidan student now living in Austria.**

All of Shaolin Kempo is built on optimizing these skills and techniques needed to beat a stronger opponent. This is how you should train. The rules and principles in the techniques and applications, that we will discuss later are key. This is the understanding you must bring to your practice in order to achieve high-level skill.

That being said, it is still your responsibility to know the laws of the land and to be in the right legally. Do not say antagonistic things. Do not follow them even for a few steps if they start to move away (no matter what they have may said). If an altercation starts use your self defense skills to safely leave. If you end up causing physical injury to the person, call the police as soon as you have reached safety to report the incident. Truly, a whole book could be written on the specifics of self defense and the law. This is not that book! It is expected that the content in Shaolin Kempo Unveiled is understood within the context of obedience to the laws of the land.

If you must resort to violence, do so with the intent to escape safely and no more. Adding a couple of body kicks when the person is down enters into the realm of criminal action. Still, the right to protect yourself and others is upheld in most countries. Do so when necessary, just do it wisely. Again and always, the best self- defense avoids physical conflict.

A DEFINITION OF SHAOLIN KEMPO KARATE

Shaolin Kempo is a martial art with diverse training for protection skills, training for professional and amateur sport fighters, for internal cultivation, health, and the development of personal responsibility and personal growth. It is a comprehensive and diversified means of unarmed self-defense, though it encompasses both an armed and unarmed system of combat with techniques (applications) of varying appearances and methods.

As a martial art, Shaolin Kempo is referred to as a Do or a Way. By this it is meant a way of being and a path towards enlightenment. "Mastering others is strength, mastering the self is true power." - Lao Tzu. This concept sums the full circle of what Shaolin Kempo strives towards. Although on its surface Shaolin Kempo can be seen as a singular form of self-defense, hidden beneath its physical exterior are levels where the cohesion of mind and body forms. At this level, Shaolin Kempo's practitioners elevate from a simple form of fighting to a higher level of ability and enlightenment.

On an external level, Shaolin Kempo is a complete fighting system of offensive and defensive methods, with equal emphasis of striking techniques with the hands and feet, immobilization and controls, projections and take downs, as well as weaponry, various spiritual and medicinal arts.

Shaolin Kempo, as developed in America, as are all of the Chow-related arts (more about Prof.Chow later), is a street-wise defensive art that does not restrict its students in methodology. Clawing hands evolve into stomping kicks. Hidden joint locks turn into disorienting and devastating takedowns. Evasive blocks turn into breath closing chokes.

The Shaolin Kempo system we teach contains 108 numbered combinations and techniques of the five animals, our system of aiki-jitsu, the unique Forms / Kata of Shaolin Kempo, as well as the Okinawa pinan / heian series, weapons defense and weapons training. The combinations and the kata make up the backbone and core of our system. We place a strong emphasis on body mechanics, structural integrity, energetic cohesion, and control, thereby allowing the art to be effective for us even when our bodies are not in peak condition. The health benefits of the internal training inherent in the system are powerful, deep and lasting.

Shaolin Kempo provides endless possibilities. The only true fighting systems are those where there are no rules applied. As early as the Han dynasty there are books that teach that nothing is impossible to a willing mind. It is from this saying that we derive the upper principles of Shaolin Kempo. What sets Kempo apart from boxing, wrestling, and other contact oriented art forms, is an emphasis on the energetic cohesion of body and mind.

Many people are quite happy with only the surface value of Kempo, taking its studies for reasons of physical health, self-defense, or a Monday night hobby. There is nothing wrong with this approach at all, yet there is more. Shaolin Kempo works to build a person's character, confidence, psychological persona and betterment. Shaolin Kempo is not solely a means of felling an opponent by force, but it teaches an inner peace to one's life and to the universe around us.

KEMPO AND KENPO, WHAT IS THE DIFFERENCE?

Kempo, also sometimes spelled "Kenpo", is a 'common' Japanese term used to refer to unarmed martial arts, and is sometimes used as a blanket term for martial arts in general. Chu'an fa is the term that is being transliterated. Typical, translated, "fist principles". As a result of grammatical rules it should be pronounced "keMpo". We have found that in North America generally the kenpo spelling tends to denote those iterations of the art that have branched from the lineage of Ed Parker. Most keMpo styles have branched from the lineage of Chow-Mitose. We note that the keMpo styles fit more closely, in terms of techniques and philosophy on movement to our sibling art of Kajukenbo, than American KeNpo. Both have distinctive elements of a common heritage while managing a clear separation.

Prof. Tom Ingargiola has traveled extensively around the United States doing seminars on Shaolin Kempo for over three decades. He has noticed the art of Shaolin Kempo being taught exactly the same way, but under different names. Some of the names have been Chinese Kempo, Chinese Kenpo, Five Animal Kempo, Shaolin kenpo, Kenpo, Kempo, American Kempo, Five Animal American Kempo, to name a few. Additionally, the same art has been taught by various organizations over the past several decades. Each organization has made slight alternations to the art or its curriculum, however the core art form of Shaolin Kempo will shine through quite vividly if one observes a class in person. Some of these organizational names are: United Studios of Self Defense, Villari's Self Defense Centers (aka Fred Villaris Studios of Self Defense), Masters of Karate, Masters Self Defense Centers, Shaolin Self Defense Centers, White Tiger Kempo, Shaolin Kempo Kung Fu, Shaolin Chu'an Fa, etc. This list in no way is meant to be an exhaustive list nor indicate any order of proficiency or merit. One could fill several pages of break-off organizations that use Shaolin Kempo as their base art. The old cliché of "A rose by any other name would still smell as sweet," applies perfectly to the situation of Shaolin Kempo organizations. The techniques have been labeled different ways by different schools, yet they are the same art and the same family, the same Ohana. Most of the above discussed variations in art/organizational names stem from commercialization and specialization of Shaolin Kempo that has occurred since it hit mainland USA. This will be discussed in greater detail later on.

Most of us have seen a kung fu movie with the good guy, or sometimes even the bad guy delivering the line: "Your kung fu is no good!". This has been interpreted often as, "Your style stinks!". Kung fu really means the time and energy one puts into perfecting a skill or talent. So the truth runs closer to a question of practice, training and development rather than the effectiveness of a particular style.

MARTIAL ART

A martial art by definition is an expression of the art of war. The root word of "martial" is Mars, or more precisely "belonging to Mars". Mars, being the mythological god of war, leads us to a definition of martial that equates with terms such as warlike, military and warrior. Although fighting systems have existed in most cultures throughout time, the term martial arts has traditionally been linked to the Asian emptied handed arts. This entails an important distinction that being the archetypical character of the martial artist and warrior. The Asian martial arts in the heritage of Shaolin Kempo developed from scholarly teachings. The term martial practice has been introduced as an alternate to "martial arts". We are persuaded by the argument that with the modern era's emphasis on scientific method and the nebulous concept of fighting as an "art", remains incomplete. However, "Martial practice" as a term is rather anaemic and "martial science" opens too many areas of criticism. Were we to change anything we would say, the "practice of martial arts". Ultimately, it is right practice that will elevate one's gung fu / kung fu and self development to the level of mastery.

The classical martial arts are usually tied to a "Way," a "Do". As the practice of martial arts spread outside the historical cultures associated with these beliefs, many modern martial art practitioners tended to exclude the esoteric and philosophical teachings as unnecessary religious trappings. Practitioners began testing their skill against one another out of ego and bravado. Then would attribute victory to particular forms and movements in their chosen style. In fact, even teachers began to believe the kata they taught and the techniques they drilled into their students were extra special in and of themselves.

The term martial arts consists of two words, martial & arts, and they cannot be separated. You cannot have one without the other when speaking of Kempo and similar fighting traditions, just as there can be no yin without yang. Our intention with this book is to give the student of Shaolin Kempo a guide for growth in this art as it is taught in our dojos; as well as a guide to development of self.

This is not a collection of techniques and forms, nor do we want it to become simply a technical manual, or the foundation of a cult like following of well-meaning practitioners prone to codification. We want to explore and share Shaolin Kempo with you, as we have come to understand it and teach it in our dojos. The forms and techniques are used to aid in the elucidation of the principles and concepts. We do not want to entice students of Shaolin Kempo to become our clones but rather our successors, taking what they have lived and practiced to the next level and imbuing the practice with their individuality.

> *"Do not try to do what you think the technique is supposed to do (turn, fell, lock ...). Simply trust the movements and it will happen...otherwise bad mechanics can result"* - **Marlon Wilson**

THE EARLY HISTORY OF SHAOLIN KEMPO

Karate

Since the time people have walked this earth there has been a need for self protection. As societies formed and people co-habited the need for skills to defend against habitual acts of violence. Human history is filled with conquerors and empires. In this way, many various fighting traditions spread across the globe. Each touch point resulted in a mingling and refinement of skill sets and traditions. The pragmatic and utilitarian nature of the need for self protection created a way of continuous improvement in the martial arts. While many cultures do not have a clear historical record of the development of their fighting traditions the Chinese Shaolin monks recount a strong narrative.

They link their history clearly to a 6th century Indian travelling Buddhist monk by the name of Bodhidharma a.k.a Damo. He travelled to China (the Middle kingdom) to bring the teachings of the Buddha to the Emperor. After his time with the Emperor Bodhidharma decided to visit the monks of Shaolin. He found them weak and infirm from their solitary dedication to meditation and spiritual development.

The travelling monk added esoteric exercises for personal and spiritual development to their regiment. These exercises also had a self defense aspect to them. The Shaolin monks resorted to them and refined them to a high level in order protect themselves. This is the beginning of the Shaolin fighting arts, Shaolin Chu'an Fa or Way of the Fist.

THE MODERN HISTORY OF SHAOLIN KEMPO

The knowledge of Kempo or Chu'an fa, was brought from China through Okinawa to Kyushu, Japan. Many generations of practitioners practiced and refined the art in times when getting it wrong could easily see you dead. It developed over the years into the modern form that is referred to as Kosho Ryu Kempo or the "old pine tree" school of Kempo.

In 1916 at the age of five, an American born Japanese boy by the name of James Mitose (December 30,1916 - March 26,1981) was sent from his home in Hawaii to his ancestral home in Japan. There he studied the family art of self defense of Kosho Ryu Kempo for fifteen years. He returned to Hawaii in 1936 a master of the art and promptly opened his Official Self-Defense Club and began teaching.

Bruce Juchnik now heads the Kosho Ryu Kempo of James Mitose. Although Hanshi Juchnik has not been directly involved in the development and lineage of Shaolin Kempo, he, as the head of Kosho Ryu, merits mention. He works tirelessly to unite all kempo styles as family to share history and techniques for self defense. The "young pine tree" school, did grow out of the "old pine tree" school after all.

William Kwai Sun Chow (July 3, 1914 - September 21,1987) studied under Mitose. Earlier, we used the term "Chow related arts" and this man is the reason. He is perhaps the epicenter of modern Kempo as we know it in the Western world. William Chow had studied his family art of kung fu and also studied several years under Mitose. Prof. Chow united his family kung fu with the Kosho Ryu Kempo he learned under Mitose and formed a new art that he initially named Kenpo Karate in order to distinguish his teachings from Mitose. He was the first to use the term "shaolin kempo" or Young Pine tree Kempo (as opposed to Kosho-Ryu Kempo or "old pine tree kempo"), although his art would eventually come to be known as Kara-Ho Kempo. In 1949, the young William Chow opened a training hall of his own. Some of the students who trained with him came from Mitose's school, including the members of the famous "Black Belt Society" who eventually formed the art of Kajukenbo. Over the years Chow blended the circular movements and principles of his family kung fu with the principles and more linear movements of Kosho ryu. He developed only a few kata and focused on core techniques to preserve and transmit his knowledge. Ed Parker, Sr., Adriano Emparado, Bill Chun, Sr., Sam Kuoha, Bobby Lowe, John Leoning, Ralph Castro, and Nick Cerio all represent legendary martial artists and others who have trained under the prolific Master William Chow.

Adriano Emparado (June 15,1926 - April 4,2009) was awarded his black belt from William Chow. He learned boxing and basic escrima from his father. Later he became part of the "black belt society" that was composed of Peter Young, Joseph Holck, Frank Ordonez, George Chuen Yoke Chang. They all trained together grafting their various arts of Tang Soo Do, boxing, Danza-ryu Jujitsu, Se Kieno-ryu judo and Sil-lum Hung Gar kung fu onto the back-bone system of the Mitose-Chow Kempo. They tested their creation in the slums of Hawaii and eventually combined the names of their arts into the name of their style: Kajukenbo.

Edmund Parker Sr. (March 19,1931 - December 15,1990) is a man who took some of the knowledge and training of Prof. Chow and made it his own. Edmund Parker is the creator of American Kenpo Karate. He was able to codify his art extensively in written form for his students to follow after him.

Walter Godin (March 21,1937 - August 7,2001) was the co-Founder of Karazenpo Go-shinjutsu with his brother-in-law Sonny Gascone. Walter Godin trained under Professor Chow and also trained in Kajukenbo under Grandmaster Adriano Emperado. Two of his most famous students are: Professor Feliciano Ferriera and Grandmaster Hackleman (Chuck "Iceman" Liddell is one of Grandmaster Hackleman's students). In 1973 Professor Chow handed down a Professorship with a 10th Degree Diploma and his blessings to Grandmaster Godin.

Sonny Gascon (March 6,1933-December 16, 2013) is the person who brought much of the kata, combinations, and techniques now seen in many styles of Kempo onto the mainland of the United States. If you are familiar with Kempo/Kenpo descriptions such as the Numbered Katas, Statue of the Crane, Combinations 1 through 26, etc., then you are a kempo descendent of Sonny Gascon. Many systems in the lineage, such as Fred Villari's Shaolin Kempo, Master's Self Defense Centers, United Studios of Self Defense, and even Professor Cerio's Kenpo are either directly or indirectly linked to Grandmaster Gascon. Two of his most notable students are Joe Blacquerra and Grandmaster George Pesare.

TO THE EAST COAST OF THE UNITED STATES

George Pesare (February 18,1939 - October 14,2012) held a 10th degree Black Belt and is responsible for bringing Kempo Karate to New England. George Pesare began his martial arts career with Karazenpo-Go-Shinjutsu in 1958 with his instructor, Grandmaster Victor (Sonny) Gascon, one of the Kempo masters who co-founded the Karazenpo Go-Shinjutsu organization and style.

Nick Cerio learned Kempo under Grand Master Pesare and trained with such notables as Prof. Chow and Ed. Parker, Sr. This is the man that introduced the Okinawan Pinan series into the system. As well, he created a completely new version of pinan number 2 and the forms Circle of Tiger, Circle of Leopard and Circle of Panther. Nick Cerio was ranked a 10th degree black belt by the World Council of Sokes, a 9th. Degree black belt from Ed Parker in Kenpo Karate, and a fifth dan by William K.S. Chow. All this knowledge and skill he developed into Nick Cerio's Kenpo. Frederick Villari studied Kenpo with Nick Cerio.

Frederick Villari became a black belt under Nick Cerio. He used the training he received from Nick Cerio, kajukenbo, and other sources of Asian kung fu to create his system of Shaolin Kempo Karate. Fred Villari formatted his teaching methods and business model quite successfully and was responsible for the opening of hundreds of martial art schools throughout the United States.

Charles Mattera first studied Kempo under Fredrick Villari. He is the Head Master of the United Studios of Self Defense. He has since studied with the Shaolin temple and was awarded Grand Master status in June 2000.

Steve DeMasco studied Shaolin Kempo under Frederick Villari and Charles Mattera. He is credited with bringing many of the weapons forms found in Shaolin Kempo to the system. Steve DeMasco continued his studies with the Shaolin Temple and was awarded Grand Master status in June 2000.

Precepts for Training and Development As a Warrior

FIRST, THE THREE MOTHERS

The three mothers are Body, Mind and Spirit. Each of the three must be trained and be governed with an end goal of the harmony of all three.

Strength, endurance, working structural integrity and suppleness are the hallmarks of good physical training. The conditioning of the Body includes, reaction drills, training against resistance, countless repetitions, bag work of some sort, having resisting partners, exercise and practicing for power. It also includes proper rest, eating well, enjoyment of life and moderation. These all promote the pursuit of excellence.

The Mind requires a relaxed state in order to function at peak levels. Success in the training of the body bridges to the training of the mind and sublimation of fear. A warrior cannot afford to fear neither death nor life, or to be paralyzed in the face of the unexpected nor, to succumb to being unfocused. A warrior remains open and receptive to ideas and thinking that differs for their own. Seek always to refine all the knowledge you have and that you find. Cultivate both sides of the brain, both the objective and the subjective sides. In most cases to achieve this, active silence is the best rule, i.e., some form of meditation.

The Spirit expresses itself most purely in infancy, albeit unrefined. The task of the warrior encompasses using the postures and training of the body and, directing the mind to stretch, enrich and refine the Spirit without diminishing its purity. We can term this, the cultivation of the self. It is no small task, and it has no end.

THE RULES OF THE DOJO

EFFORT - Effort begins before the class starts and continues on well after the class has ended. Excellence depends on the effort given. While many enjoy early success because of sheer physical talent, it can take them only so far. We all can recall a student with crazy skills, who could pick up a new move in a breath and execute it as though being born to it. At the advanced levels, the demands go beyond mere mimicry and soon, to everyone's shock and dismay, the student quits. Many cannot reconcile the level of effort now needed to be given as an advanced belt with their immature idea of what constitutes a good martial artist. Discouragement sets in and in the end, such students leave not only the school but martial arts in general.

We would say, partially a failure on our part as instructors and also, not everyone wants to or is willing to do what it takes to truly master the art of Shaolin Kempo.

ETIQUETTE - Each training place follows explicit or implicit formalities. These range from dress code, acceptable and unacceptable language, chain of command, and ritual. First and foremost etiquette is about a mindset. The essentials of getting the most for your effort stems from the mindset you keep while training. This extends through actions into thought. By no means can we expect a student not to question. Do not misconstrue etiquette in this manner. Rather, extrapolate the notion of effort to an immersion of self into the ethos or paradigm of ones chosen art. The head of the style creates the tone and the chief instructor "flavors" it with her/his personality. Yet, all remains within the boundaries of the wū shih-do or

būshi-do of the system. There is a "way" of conduct that the practitioner of Shaolin Kempo is expected to maintain. Either it expresses itself through the etiquette in and out of the dojo or the student only advances so far.

CHARACTER - Character or integrity is who we are and what we do when we cannot be seen or have consequences forced on us. Effort and etiquette can be imposed on a person through external influence. Character, or rather the desired character, internalizes the fertile groundwork of effort and etiquette and so, grows into something more. Character differentiates a mere brute, even a highly skilled brute from a warrior. Character defines a warrior.

CONTROL - Becoming a warrior begins and ends with control. First, control of the body, equilibrium and breath. Then, control of the will, mind and the spirit leading to the control of others. Culminating in the control of one's life and the ability to truly be free, let go and advance. Before one can control another in a self-defense situation, one must learn to control themselves, both physically, mentally, and emotionally.

SELF-DISCIPLINE - None of the above will lead to any lasting or significant results without discipline of the self. Discipline is a state of order and growth based on submission to rules and authority either external or internal, often both. Training and dedication will bring the student from following the external demands of the teacher for discipline to a point where the impetus becomes internal. Self-discipline extends beyond the routine of regular training, it is the will that one applies to bring the knowledge, teachings, and thinking coherently to every aspect of one's life. Discipline can be imposed externally. Self-discipline comes from within. The true Shaolin Kempo practitioner always strives to be self-disciplined.

EXTEND TO LIFE

SEEK KNOWLEDGE - Shaolin Kempo follows a logic of movement and flow that reflects a way of thinking. As students delve into understanding Shaolin Kempo, we begin to recognize a coherence in the system that follows a powerful logic. Truth tends not to be limited and so one can expect this logic to exist outside of Shaolin Kempo training. A student will not only begin to recognize such things, they will seek them out. They will deepen their thinking of the art to the point where they will see Kempo everywhere: in everyday life, academic studies, business, sports, art..., etc. Works such as "The book of Five Rings" and "The Art of War" used in business, are examples of the knowledge of martial arts applying to other aspects of life. The above mentioned books are written works and Shaolin Kempo is a living work. The student, hungry for all good things, will read outside of the martial arts also. They will read and learn of poetry, novels, history, science, classic and modern arts, theatre, movies. They will learn skills, not only from other styles but outside of martial arts as well. They will attend seminars, learn other languages and use the internet and community to continually grow and develop as a warrior. As always, conscious and conscientious that not everything written or said is true. Students of Shaolin Kempo will educate themselves and share with others along the way.

COMMUNITY - Hegel, the 19th century German philosopher of Idealism said that anyone existing outside of a community is either a demon or a god. Judeo-Christian wisdom states that no one (man) is an island. Warriors do not exist solely for themselves. They exist for family and community even if that does not extend beyond the dojo at first. In our style, the higher ranks of 7th, 8th, and 9th dan contain a community requirement. That is to say that to obtain these ranks a contribution must have been made. This is the highest level of being a warrior. To give back in a meaningful manner, not simply to our art, but to our family and the larger community.

The Five Animals of Shaolin Kempo

Shaolin Kempo advocates a five animal system. Train in order to learn from the animal strategies and techniques not to merely imitate them!

THE TIGER - STRENGTH, TENACITY, FEROCITY

Claw strikes, tiger palms, tiger mouth strikes are associated with this style of fighting. The tiger is known for using the attributes of a low center of gravity and body weight to its advantage. There is a strong emphasis on locking joints, ripping muscle and tendons with devastating effects on an attacker. The tiger is simple, honest and direct. The tiger style represents dominance, strength, power and action, thereby overwhelming an opponent with superior force.

THE LEOPARD - SPEED, POWER, AGILITY

Leopard paw strikes, elbows, forearms, knees, coupled with quick shifting motions from the waist distinguishes the leopard. Another characteristic of the leopard is powerful driving blows that keep an attacker uprooted. The leopard does not carry as much mass as the tiger, therefore it cannot crush its prey as a tiger does. Instead, it relies on speed, and agility to compensate. The leopard attacks with a relentless series of strikes. Unlike the tiger, the leopard has less use for deep rooted stances. The leopard style of fighting itself, roots only momentarily for power generation and for quick leaps and directional changes off of a strong, yet mobile base.

THE CRANE - GRACE, BALANCE, PATIENCE

Characteristic strikes are the crane strike / chicken wrist, the cranes beak, wing strike, front kick, blade kick, and snap kicks. The Crane possesses the ability to grip the ground for balance, chooses to deflect most blows by creating angles with its footwork to compliment deflecting and redirecting blocks. Uniquely graceful, light and patient, the crane style reinforces watching and waiting and so, rarely initiates an attack. The crane evades and when judged appropriate, it acts. The Crane will find vital points to counterstrike such as the eyes, nose, ears, the crown of the head or any target suitable for its long reach and strong beak. The crane generally counters from any angle except for squarely in front. It side steps or angles off then counters with its attack hidden by its movement.

THE SNAKE - INNER / COORDINATED, ACCUMULATED POWER (CHI), PRECISION, SUPPLENESS

The snake moves and strikes with precision, order, and endurance in a coordinated manner that is strictly defined in order to maximize the expression of power or fajin. The snake strikes with finger pokes, spear hand strikes, snake bites and deceptive kicks. The snake stance prepares coiling power for release. The style focuses on speed, suppleness, knowledge, timing, precision and pressure points strikes with associated sequences. At a distance the snake is a viper. Much like the crane, the viper bides its time, waiting for the right moment and the right target for a precision attack. Up close this snake becomes a constrictor. Using deception and stillness, the constrictor capitalizes on contact to trap, wrap and crush the attacker, as well as straining ligaments, joints and breaking bones. This aspect of the snake fighting easily creates locks and chokes to disable the attacker. The snake incorporates more evasion than blocking, employing more bobs, weaves and slips than direct blocks. It relies on agility and quick reflexes to avoid contact, aside from when it chooses to advance for counter-attacks.

THE DRAGON - RIDES THE WIND, FIGHTING SPIRIT, TRANSCENDENCE

The dragon uses any hand strike, spinning kicks, multiple kicks and uses whipping motions powered by rotation generated through the waist. In many oriental legends, <Insert dragon image, word wrap> the dragon often arrives with a storm cloud and can strike like the wind and lightning, from all directions. There are many rising and falling motions in the dragon that represent the motion of smoke and wind.

Some consider the dragon as the "fifth element" unifying the other four animal styles into one. Although the dragon has its preferred weapons, the legend of its shape-shifting ability is demonstrated by the fighter using all the weapons of the other animals in an adaptive and indomitable manner. The dragon fights with wisdom.

The animals represent distinct ways of fighting. Most people will find themselves gravitating to one particular animal due to body type and personal preference. However, Shaolin Kempo represents the power of adaptability, so we strive to learn and master each way of fighting. Especially since a self defense situation may determine that the best response comes from a combination of strategies. These are taught right from the beginning, and at green belt we begin to focus on an animal per belt in preparation for shodan first degree black belt.

The Basics

RELAXATION

An incredibly important part of the basics is learning to relax. This often presents a difficulty in Shaolin Kempo as the art starts out focusing on self defense and in many ways as a hard karate style. The relaxation needed extends to the fascia and ligaments. As the students relax, they "lengthen their muscles" promoting increased circulation of blood and a lengthening of the fascia. This extent of relaxation promotes the internal and external coordination that is essential for listening, proper release of energy (fa jing) and, ultimately control when engaged with an attacker. Let's face it though, developing true martial skill resulting from such alignment and relaxation, while simply standing still, takes time to master. The coordination necessary to move with alignment and with proper SONG (relaxation) takes years.

So Shaolin Kempo compensates with some hard hitting, intelligently designed techniques that will work well enough with strength, technique and directness for the beginner. They tense up, scream, punch hard, kick hard and move hard. In the end, they learn many things that will save them, if attacked. Enter, stun, unbalance, control, cross and cover and be ready for the next bad guy. Most students love this stage and most instructors enjoy their enthusiasm. We all learn from this initial beginner stage and at the same time, can't wait until it's over so the real training can begin in earnest. This is why we stress relaxation amidst, the intensity of the youth driven craving to conquer. We stress relaxation while demanding more push ups, better squats and lower stances. We stress relaxation because we know that in order to elevate athleticism to an art we must move beyond aggression and angst into harmony and understanding. All mastery presents itself with a characteristic ease. The seemingly effortless movements of a Michael Jordan, or the strokes of a master painter or a master chef or a song writer, all show us that there exists something beyond the steps of "doing it right". All show us a place we would love to go to with our chosen passions and our lives.

This begins and ends with relaxation and unceasing devotion and practice.

STRUCTURAL INTEGRITY

The aspect of structural integrity allows one to survive the initial attack, move effectively, strike powerfully and control yourself and the situation. Ultimately, the ability to return home to your family and friends safe and sound is the paramount fundamental! This requires structural integrity.

These are the basics of the basics: A strong root in the legs, a solid core and spinal alignment. To align the spine the head must feel as though it is being pulled upwards, NOT PUSHED, while the tailbone sits under the center of the head and yet feels as though it is sinking downwards. The spine can still be misaligned if the back is not rounded. The shoulders and elbows must be down. Relax into the position and unlock the knees. Keep the toes pointed in line with the knees and remember the alignment of shoulders-hips, elbows-knees, and hands-feet. **Relaxation and staying alert are things that we in the West do not associate together.**

Let gravity hold you up and allow the secondary muscles to come into play as needed and pay attention to your body. Start by focusing on your breathing: Exhale with the mouth as the diaphragm pushes downward and inhale through the nose, easy and unforced. Gently press the tongue to the roof of the mouth, slightly behind the top front teeth. Keep your attention on the center point in the middle of your torso at the height of approximately two finger widths below the navel. Let your joints be open and not tight especially in the pelvic area and the ankles. Sink and relax. Relaxing in this context is to allow yourself to expand into the six directions (up, down, left, right, front and back), while lengthening your fascia and tendons. "Relax" (SONG) is an essential basic. Of course this all must be worked on while you are still, and then after a certain level of mastery, it must be applied with movement. First in the breathing exercises and then ultimately, applied at all times.

All throughout your training we are sure that time and again you have heard it said that nothing you learn is effective without the basics. Many masters have been asked what their secret is or what tips they had to offer for advancement. The answer is always the same: Focus on the basics. It seems obvious and we agree. Many will tell you that it is mere repetition that will bring the seemingly magical abilities we all began training in the martial arts to achieve. However, it is **right practice that brings you to perfection, not mere blind repetition.**

Ok, so back to the basics. Before anything else there is structural integrity and leg strength. After that there is leg strength and structural integrity. While doing everything else there is structural integrity and leg strength. Many martial arts classes use the horse stance with the beginners a great deal. The reason we use horse stance training is to build leg strength and an easy way to check alignment. Squats and zhan zhoung (standing meditation / training) are excellent starters as well. Squats are great because in addition to building the leg strength, they help develop core muscles, flexibility and open the pelvis area nicely and they exercise you in a way that is beneficial to the cardiovascular system and muscle tone.

The standing allows you to listen to your body and learn to feel it. If you do not have the quiet stillness, it becomes much harder to notice when you are not aligned and if you do not notice you cannot self correct. Zhan Zhoung (a standing qi gong exercise to develop internal power) trains something of extreme importance as well. It trains what is called in Chinese internal arts "SONG", that suppleness and lengthening of joint, sinew and muscle that allows true speed and power to develop.

Zhan Zhoung Front View Side View

BREATHING

Breath is life. The Taiji classics teach that a baby is the perfect and complete example of qi, this gets overlooked as a child (uncultivated and spent) and then, one spends the rest of their adult life trying to return back to the perfect balance bestowed upon them at birth. Any discussion of breathing is a conversation about life force and thus can be properly termed qi gong. Qi gong cultivates suppleness, vitality and energy in the body. The health benefits are powerful and well documented. It requires that time and energy be persistently and consistently applied. The work, the gong fu or Kung fu of qi gong can be seated, standing still or in motion. It is the cultivation of breath through abdominal breathing. It is relaxed, centered and grounded. Attention is given to the sensations, feelings and "path" of the breath and qi. Once attention becomes intention, the work involves "leading" the qi, the gong fu is properly termed nei gong. Again this can be worked seated, standing still, and moving.

Study the energy channels or simply begin with the Conception and Governor channels, at first.

Conception And Governor Channels

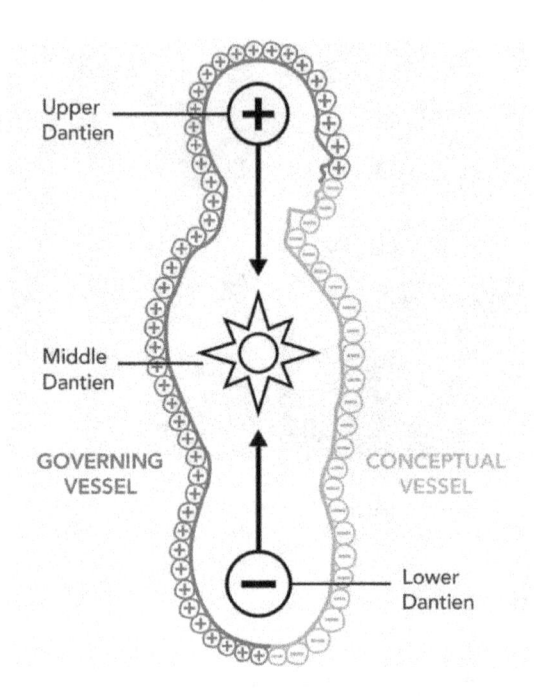

The exercises appear simple and that adds to the challenge of consistency and persistence. They are also quite precise, seek a knowledgeable teacher. One cannot arrive at the highest point without beginning the journey to the mountain. Remember, **"a journey of a thousand miles begins with a single step"**.

Shaolin Kempo adapts to the internal path as easily as the external path. In some ways one can describe the difference being in one's attention. When your focus draws from your interior then your practice leans in an internal style direction.

When your focus draws from outside yourself, then the term external more properly applies. Breath cultivation, internal listening, then learning to lead your energy with your intention, will enrich your martial arts training and development. Such practices open the way for you to achieve higher skill levels.

If you do not develop the ability to visualize to a high degree, your progress and growth towards mastery will have a low ceiling.

The Rising Sun is a great introductory breathing exercise. The basics of legs, alignment, sinking, relaxation and breath are worked together along with upper body movement that teaches some important mechanics. The waist guides the power that is found by pushing into the ground.

Through the heel the impetus comes on the inhalation and is separated at the waist with a rise and forward circular motion (small) of the center point, into the two arms. They circle outwards but NOT behind until the hands are above the head and the elbows do not rise above the shoulders. Form a triangle at the level of the heart and exhale as the triangle extends out from the body. At the end of the breath once again push down with the heels on inhalation and the waist separates the arms outwardly as cranes, this time with a rise and a backward circular motion of the center point. The elbows remain unlocked and the shoulders remain loose, down and open. As the breath leaves, the hands rotate outwards forming knife / sword hands touch at the end of the breath. Once again push with the feet and allow the one point to direct the wrists upwards with a forward rotation of the one point and on exhalation the hands descend in the form of tiger claws. Repeat 2 more times.

On inhalation stay relaxed and add tension when exhaling. The tension moves from being the whole body to gradually and in stages, being only in the part of the hand being used as a weapon. Lastly, we arrive at not expressing tension at all and, only energy. The mind leads the qi. It is difficult to explain qi. To be honest, it may be better to not think of it as an objective thing. Subjectively, the term qi or chi, expresses a force that holistically allows for the psycho-physiological manifestation of power beyond the expected. The time and energy used to develop this skill, this power, is the kung fu of our system more than any animal technique or form.

Eventually we shorten, bit by bit, the intake of breath as we relax the abdomen enough that a full breath sinks easily and quickly. Keep the mind centered at the center point, even as it leads the qi to the hands and feet. This is done in stages and should not be pushed. Take your time and listen to your body as you do this exercise. This is a major part of the internal. Remember to understand and master the Yang you must understand and master the Yin (please see page 4).

THE WAIST DRIVES THE POWER

The next basic we concentrate on is the use of the waist. Whereas driving your weight into the ground gives you power (this is also a function of SONG), it is the waist that needs to direct and amplify this power. Partly because your center point resides in the waist, and also because this is the center of your body. The difference between the two is that the center point is a place of transformation of energy and the center of your body is purely an anatomical location. **The waist directs the power.** If this principle is not followed then you are using strength alone, which is much less efficient. Many instructors exaggerate a wiggle when teaching the use of the waist. It can look quite funny to do so and is therefore more memorable. Keep in mind that this movement can easily be misinterpreted in two ways. First only as moving side to side. There is, in fact, a much more complex and robust action happening. Second, the movement may look as though it is confined to the hips. The waist comprises the torso from the bottom of the rib cage to the pelvis.

When one sinks into the earth and finds power rising up it can simply expand or be directed to a specific purpose. Breathing is essential here, but must not limit the expression of power. The triangle and the lever, and the crisscross pattern of energy distribution all can come into play. Always remember that **what is primary resides in the knowledge and practice of using the waist to direct power.**

Prof. Ingargiola, my teacher, once made a sound (something like brrrvr-dom!) as he "whipped" his spine forward and dropped his weight while executing a punch for me when I asked how he was able to generate such power in his strikes. It was one of the best commentary of the taiji classics I had ever encountered. Visualize: It is as though whipping a string of pearls into that one moment of power; or a magician flicking a string and it turning into a wand. At another time when he explained the form Tai Sing Mon to me he completed the circle and deepened my understanding. The key point in opening or closing as an expression of power lies in the coordination and guidance of the waist. This cannot be accomplished being fixated on force.

One error we recognize repeatedly while engaging the waist is the lack of return. People push their hip out to one side and keep the off-balance, non-relaxed stance while screaming. This is both ugly and incomplete, and inefficient. One key is to generate power through **one point on your opponent's body** with contact to **one point** on your body at **ONE POINT IN TIME**. Exaggerated or extended hip movement tends to make one lose the recoil/snap of the motion and the physical and mental power generated gets dissipated over a period of time. Remember, IT'S ONE POINT ON THEIR BODY> ONE POINT ON YOUR BODY> AT ONE POINT IN TIME!!!

Here is another way to think of recoil and rest. Picture working a wrist lock and only focusing on the push element of the lock with no focus on the recoil or the return to your center.

Side note from Master Wilson:

I recall teaching a wrist lock to a student once, and after I explained and demonstrated, left them to practice while I checked in on some others. I was soon called back...it wasn't working. I had the student show me what they were doing and saw the error immediately. The student used too much strength because their partner had a size advantage. In the end however, all they succeeded in accomplishing was to push the arm away from them at the cost of considerable effort. Only the "return" lacked in their technique. When they brought a circle to that push and returned towards their own center with the wrist, the effect was startlingly dramatic and almost effortless.

Always strive to return to equilibrium. Return to a state of rest because that is where our truth resides. Rest and equilibrium are the basics. So this is the waist. Will we generate power or lose power from our waist action? The waist can be a generator of power or a constrictor of power. The key to making our waist become a power generating machine is homework and practice followed by more homework and more practice. We seek to perfect our practice because, **only perfect practice will make your practice perfect.**

Tool Kit of Strikes

Remember that once we are unavoidably faced with a fight, our every thought, our presence, our actions and our focused intent is to escape unharmed. Our goal is to return home safe and sound. At the point where avoidance, de-escalation and retreat have not been fruitful, we need to engage effectively, efficiently and powerfully. Choose the tools that not only suits the best intention of controlling the situation, and matches the opportunity, but also one that delivers the right energy / jin for your intent. The energy (jin) to uproot, draw in, redirect, pull down, grab, push, press, fold, throw, drop, break, penetrate, or release. To be clear, when we strike the goal is not purely offensive, not only to cause damage. Rather, it is contact…CONTACT = CONTROL = WINNING. We must seek to disrupt the attacker's equilibrium, balance, musculoskeletal system and center. There is a science and technique to this practice and it is all in our combinations, kempos, animal techniques and forms. In depth observation of ourselves and our practice partners will help us continually raise our skill level. Here, we list some of the traditional empty hand combat weapons. What is the energy or are the goals of each?

The hammer fist (dropping, cross, reverse, driving); the front punch; the thrust punch; the jab; the leopard paw; the bear paw; the back punch; the upper cut; the hook punch; the dragon head strike; the trigger finger; the poke (single finger, two finger, immortal man, spear); the palm heel, willow, Buddha; the knife hand, reverse, driving; the tiger claw, mouth, eagle; the crane's head / chicken wrist strike; the front kick and heel kick; the back kick; the side kick, thrust and blade; the shuffling, rear cross over and front cross over kicks; the snap kick; the crescent kicks; the roundhouse, traditional and kempo; the hook kick; the dragon stomp; *the scissor kick; the stepping stool kick; the butterfly kick; spinning and jumping kicks.*

In Kempo we tend not to kick high. As many masters have stated, with the opponent bent or on the ground, this is the best method to kick to the head. We practice high kicks and "flying kicks" for flexibility and fighting spirit but we know rarely are they the optimal choice in a fight. Using our lower limbs into the ribs, legs, knees, ankles and groin area are heavily emphasized in Shaolin Kempo for striking, trapping, control of and felling an opponent.

STANCES

Let's bring our attention to the stances now, as no real discussion of the basics can be made without giving thought and practice to this foundational step. Remember the words of Professor Ingargiola, "Stances are important and we need to discuss them, however stances are positions we move through in order to accomplish goals". A stance for the sake of a stance is weak, stances help us achieve goals. Stances are offensive and defensive weapons!

A fighter needs mobility, therefore no matter the stance and no matter the weight distribution applied you must always be ready to move. Mobility has less to do with a 50-50 weight distribution than with the type of positioning that permits quick shifts and easy movement. In this sense being mobile represents a state of mind and preparedness more accurately than it does weight distribution. We do not teach to fight from a stance, rather to fight using stances. We float and move constantly. Yet, without an understanding of stances and weight distribution the achievement of high level skill will remain elusive.

Horse Stance

The Horse Riding stance, a.k.a. the Horse stance: This stance is used primarily to build a strong foundation and root. Please note that in a fight there may be a reason to use a horse stance, even though it is not a stance to "square off" with against an attacker. Of course, we practice proper spinal alignment and utilization of the waist with the Horse stance as well. The feet are positioned a little wider than shoulder width apart. The tip of the tail bone is aligned with the center of the top of the skull. It is essential that the buttock is not sticking out. The toes are pointed forwards and the knees are pressing outwards. The weight distribution starts with a 50-50 ratio. Only go as low as you can while maintaining the essentials of posture. Do not allow the knees to extend beyond the toes. Breathe regularly and evenly as you continually tell your muscles to relax. There is no benefit to bend the legs past 90 degrees.

Forward Stance

The Forward stance easily forms from the Horse stance by turning one foot 90 degrees allowing the hips to follow (the rotation of the hips is important). The heels remain in line with each other and the other foot shift anywhere between 35 – 45 degrees in the same direction. What is now the back leg remains in an unlocked position and your center point and forward foot are pointed in the same direction. The weight distribution is more on the front leg and, again, the principles of alignment must be adhered to in this and all the stances. The back leg is the main piston for power generation in the forward stance. Part of the reason we do not lock the back leg is that Shaolin Kempo uses a great deal of mobility as a fighting system and in a fight all stances are transitional. We use a forward stance to express power forwards and we move through a target. There are other uses that are based on positioning and manipulation of your opponent's body. This is true of all stances. We will not repeat it for each stance. Do not underestimate the important aspects of your stances.

Cat Stance

The Cat stance has a straight line from the back heel to the hips through the spine to the head. The back foot is positioned at a 45 degree angle from the front and carries all the weight of the body, the front foot places the ball of the foot lightly on the ground in line with the heel of the back leg and the knee of the front leg guards access to the groin. The weight distribution ranges from 100% on the back leg and 0% weight on the front to a 90% to 10% ratio. The waist faces forwards. The stance allows for the interception of incoming force with ease while allowing the Kempo practitioner to fight close to the attacker.

Crane Stance

The crane stance or flamingo stance primarily trains balance. Almost all of our kicks move through this stance. Our goal as a multiple striking system includes continuous fighting from wherever we find ourselves without the necessity or luxury of re-setting. In this stance we seek the place of equilibrium within ourselves without the benefit of both legs on the ground, nor with compensation from our arms. Stillness and breath leads us to greater control of ourselves, which will translate into greater ability to control situations and attackers.

Half-Moon Stance

In the half-moon stance (a.k.a the fighting stance) you should strive for a relaxed stance. It is somewhat akin to a boxer's stance but with the rear leg kept grounded. Think of it a very prepared athletic stance that allows you to be able to move in any direction with intent without the need to first redistribute your weight. When you can block, punch, kick and move in any direction quickly from your fighting stance, then you are well on your way to beginning to understand how to be fluid, yet grounded. Think of the taiji, the yin yang symbol. The symbol contains both elements, the hard and the soft... the fluid and the rigid... in and out... We could go on and on with all the possibilities as to how yin and yang can manifest itself, however what is critically important to remember from this chapter is that **your fighting stance should maximize your action/reaction potential …not limit it!**

The fighting stance is mobile and well balanced allowing for easy execution of all of one's weapons and angles of escape/attack/entry. More importantly this stance provides the structural integrity to survive the initial attack in an instant, while simultaneously preparing us to be ready to respond.

Prof. Ingargiola teaches a definition of Shaolin Kempo: **"Continuous destructive motion off a powerful yet mobile base with multiple strikes, while simultaneously manipulating the opponents upper and lower body mass until the threat is over"**. We do not stand still and fight. The practice of stances is the practice of maintaining the basics while moving into different positions as you gain control of a dynamic situation. The practice of stances in a drill, the forms, and solo techniques, during embu* or against a resisting attacker during reaction drills all reinforce and hone the use of active and pragmatic stances in practical self defense. If your ability to respond remains in the dojo or only when your instructor asks for it, then it is not fully integrated and may not show up when you need it most.

*Embu is a slow motion fighting practice that can be gradually ramped up in speed as one progresses.

BLOCKING

Shaolin Kempo teaches the eight-point blocking to beginners with exaggerated movements that ensures that all blocks cover our own centerline. The Centerline theory is of the upmost importance in Shaolin Kempo. We block in order to 'cover' the center line of our body. This is because we recognize that maximum damage is usually accomplished by allowing the opponent access to our center line. The opposite is equally true, our strikes should focus on accessing our opponent's center line.

The eight point system begins as closed handed blocks. Of course, there is the essential double block/windmill block/sun-moon block. Then we teach open handed eight point blocking. We have 4-point blocking, ten point blocking, dragon blocking and the Plum Tree blocking system which leads to the Eleven Hands of Buddha! There are schools with some other complementary systems of blocking, yet these are the base systems of blocking, parrying, deflection and control in Shaolin Kempo.

All blocking practice needs to reflect the concept of control, cutting through the centerline, and the explosive power necessary for breaking, with a partner and in our practice time alone as well. Your center line gives you an axis to turn and pivot on with balance, it holds your equilibrium and without it safeguarded, your defense and offense weakens. Our Shaolin Kempo system is designed to disrupt the centerline and equilibrium of an attacker. With this simple understanding, translated into practice you will see your Shaolin Kempo's efficiency skyrocket from what you were previously able to accomplish. **Practice to keep your centerline guarded and disrupt the opponent's centerline at all times.** Remember this as you apply your stances, blocks and strikes.

A powerful key is to remember that **a block is contact and contact is control.** Control is the manipulation and direction of the opponent's musculoskeletal system, balance and focus. If you do not create control of the opponent, you have wasted energy and time in other words your kung fu. Always remember that the term 'kung fu', literally means **time** and **energy**.

Another key point to take from this chapter is that A BLOCK CAN BE A STRIKE AND A STRIKE CAN BE A BLOCK. If you have spent a decent amount of time in any Kempo school you will invariably hear this statement often, however it is often not actually practiced to make it applicable. You must work this concept on a training partner and on a striking bag as well. Take a hint from the great warrior

Miyamoto Musahi from his Book of Five Rings. The book goes into detail about acquiring the most offensive attitude when executing a defensive move and about acquiring the most defensive attitude when executing the most offensive move. It goes back to the yin yang symbol... **you cannot have one without the other!**

Rising Block   Rising Block used offensively

Authors side note:

This same concept of using "blocks" offensively is demonstrated in "What Is True Self Defense" by James Mitose.

The Weapons

Our first and greatest weapon will always be our mind. Think first! It is said that,"Karate is the first strike"(Motobu, Choki). This intends that by training and gaining mastery over our body, mind and development, our preparedness will first and foremost see that we are not unnecessarily, placing ourselves in a situation that requires fighting. Conversely, in such a situation our thinking and preparedness affords us an overwhelming advantage.

Some of you might have thought this section was going to be about weapons such as the staff or sai or tonfa. Many kempo schools do teach various traditional weaponry. There are countless weapons that can be taught. The key to remember is that the weapon in your hand is an extension of you. Some will say that this is wrong and an oversimplification of the discussion of traditional weaponry training. However, the weapon is wielded by you and your stance, your breath, your focus, your relaxation or lack of it. Everything we discussed in the basics section of this book and every fighting strategy and insight is irrevocably intertwined with the training of traditional weaponry. Hence the adage : **Training is truth, and remember YOUR MOST LETHAL WEAPON IS YOUR MIND!**

* *

Sharpening Your Most Lethal Weapon

In our fast paced culture, ruled by texting and instant messaging, there is a tendency to cut corners by skipping activities perceived to be unnecessary or too tedious. Unfortunately, this attitude now pervades the martial arts. Quite often, financial pressure on schools mandates assembly line training through which instructors push their students up the belt ranks at a quicker pace. Some unscrupulous or short-sighted martial artists have even developed methods of teaching that are less than ideal for the average person who desires to learn street- level self-defense.

What gets lost is the ability of the practitioner to internalize the knowledge and techniques they acquire from any given martial art, whether MMA, Shotokan, or even boxing. This transcends the dojo, the gym and the kwoon because it involves your most lethal weapon: your mind. Let's sharpen it!

Any body builder will tell you that you must continuously stimulate your muscles with new regiments and sequences to induce growth and development. The same holds true for your brain! Applied to your martial arts training, sharpening your mind will enhance your natural instincts and reactions for actual street defense. This section proposes five rules, and subsequent training tips, to develop and engage the mind in martial art work-outs as much as one does the body.

Rule 1-Class action must not always begin with a verbal command.

Most of your typical martial arts students develop habits in their training that run counter to the ultimate goal of learning self-defense. The trainee spends considerable amounts of time performing prearranged movements established by a given school's curriculum. As a result, the student becomes an expert at executing movements on command. In training this way, the student and his or her partner know what move to expect and when to start or finish. This approach is necessary at the outset to teach control and technique. However, an individual's practice must diverge at some point, like the proverbial child learning to ride a bike without training wheels.

Let's illustrate why this is so important:

An instructor is at the front of a room and there are two lines of students facing each other. When the teacher shouts a command, one side grabs the other in a front choke hold. As this training continues, it usually falls into a certain call/ response cadence.

The problem here is the surprise. There is NONE! Everyone is conditioned to respond on cue. Students must develop beyond this rote method once they have learned the basics. The reason: their instructors won't be there to call out moves in an actual street confrontation. Without advancing, the student ingrains the bad habit of reacting only to verbal stimuli.

(Training tip~ Employ loud noises or no noise > use physical actions to initiate reactions)

Rule 2-Never allow time to pass when hands are placed on your body.

Consider the aforementioned example a bit further and you will notice another less obvious, but equally debilitating habit being imbedded into the student's neural pathways. The side representing the victim remains passive, allowing the side playing attacker to place arms in the front choke hold before any counter is initiated. Once again, the defending side typically waits until an instructor commands a reaction.

Just as before, this scenario sends a poor message to the student's brain. This one says, "It's okay to allow someone to place their hands on my throat". It goes without saying that this is bad, VERY BAD! The brain should not be conditioned to be comfortable with someone placing their hands or arms around the throat. Like the hand that snaps back from touching a hot stove, the student's mind should habituate instant ACTION when a choke hold is attempted.

(Training Tip-Do all thinking and planning before you allow your training partner to place their hands on you. When you feel contact, your reaction is always ACTION!)

Rule 3-Always scan your environment for other adversaries and escape avenues.

This rule involves a completely different scenario, one of multiple assailants. It is imperative to train your mind to be ready for a possible next attacker. In fact, it is most prudent to always assume there is more than one. Unfortunately, what happens in most schools is that students look to their instructor for approval or critique immediately after completing a move. This is bad cerebral habituation.

You should train your mind to instinctively **survey the entire environment with a guarded mental and physical attitude.** This includes being aware of other adversaries and avenues of escape. In our schools, we allow students and assistants to "inform" their classmates of their lack of scanning with a friendly punch or grab.

(Training Tip-You must visualize 360 degrees after completing a technique. This is a major part of the intent of the "cross and cover" as well as escaping.)

Rule 4-Whenever possible, add realism to your bag work routines

You can also sharpen your brain's reaction by varying your individual bag work. We all have seen, or even been that person who counts punches or kicks to reach the number called out by the instructor. There always seems to be a race to the finish. Again, this is the wrong mindset. It should not be focused on the attainment of a particular number. After learning how to throw a particular strike, it is time to challenge your brain. Visualize an attacker, employ an initial block, or throw multiple strikes. Apply the concept from Rule #1 by using reaction to motion or a loud sound to each sequence of strikes.

Additional Training Tip-Try standing in front of a heavy bag in a darkened room with a television behind you. Every time the television changes scenery there will be a flash of light and you need to throw your sequence. Try doing bag work with a partner who holds a handheld bag while you close your eyes > your partner moves > when you hear a loud noise you open your eyes and scan your environment > you move towards the bag and strike it multiple times. By the way, the bag could be behind you. It can and should be anywhere! Not all street self-defense occurs right in front of you.

Rule # 5-Role Play, Role Play, Role Play

Role playing is a great tool to enhance your brain's ability to apply the knowledge and skills you learn. Yelling, pushing and pulling while practicing a move adds realism. The more realistic the settings are for possible attacks, the better chance you have of reacting, rather than thinking! As with the application of the other rules and tips in this section, realism should only be added after a basic understanding and application of a particular technique has been demonstrated. Your brain must internalize the stimulus-response reaction.

(Training Tips-Train outdoors in alleyways, by cars, near fences, etc. Wear work clothes or social clothing. Train in limited lighting. Train on less than ideal surface settings, i.e., uneven, wet, snow, etc. Initiate your moves from a sitting position.)

Science has demonstrated that the brain must be exercised, like any muscle in the body. Just as there are many ways to apply the maxims of the martial arts to life, this is a case of applying a fact of life to your martial arts training. This section offers only a few of the many different ways one can use to deepen their mental training. It will not only sharpen your greatest weapon, your mind, but it will make your work outs fly as well. Most people set a clock to ensure they get the right amount of exercise. When we train, we set a clock to remind ourselves to stop. Our hope is that you too, might lose track of time as you gain greater insight.

Authors side note:

Weight training is a legitimate way for a martial artist to build strength. Professor Ingargiola has a great DVD on weight training specifically tailored for martial artists if you are interested in exploring weight training. His DVD is entitled "Weightlifting for the Zen Minded".

Shaolin Kempo Weaponry Training

Each weapon can and does teach you more about your body and how to generate power. Each weapon can and does teach you how to defend against it or something similar. If you know how to use weapons you are better prepared to defend against them. The staff teaches a greater understanding of the push and pull concept between the right and left sides of your body.

A staff form is a great workout and can help develop strength, coordination and flexibility. A staff can always be mimicked in the street by a broom handle, fence post, metal rod.

We could go on and on about each weapon and its use in your training. The list below is not meant to be all inclusive or indicate any order of suggested training.

1. Sai promotes fluidity and relaxation of the shoulders, elbows and wrists in your hand striking motions. It is useful in helping one better understand the offensive and defensive use of mid-range weapons. Think liquid steel!
2. Nunchaku promotes fluidity and relaxation of the shoulders; and heightened eye-hand coordination.
3. Chinese broadsword works distance and range and as well as directing power or energy through the wrist.
4. Tonfa practices small circle power and weight transfer through strikes.
5. Archer's bow emphasizes focus and intent from a distance, breath and relaxation.
6. Escrima sticks concentrates on the flow of continuous striking and use of both hands.
7. Katana trains commitment to fully execute.
8. Dagger / Knives trains close quarter fighting and use of both hands.

If your instructor is training you in the use of a traditional weapon and you do not understand how it fits into your training, you should ask the question. The only dumb question is the unasked question. If you do not get a satisfactory answer, ask again while speaking to the instructor in private. If the answer still makes no sense to you. Perhaps it is time to move onto another school. You can learn Shaolin Kempo without training in weaponry, however your training can be expanded and become more diverse and more applicable more quickly through weapons training. The one downside of weaponry training is that you begin to focus too much on the weaponry and do not develop your basic foundation. There is an old saying that goes as such, "The tree that grows too tall without strong roots, falls at the first strong wind". Remember, YOU CANNOT HAVE THE YIN WITHOUT THE YANG! Advanced knowledge is great, but not at the expense of a solid foundation!

Strategy & Tactics

THE FIGHTING STYLE OVERVIEW

The term Kempo often translates as fist way or fist law (chu'an fa) and accounts for some justification to the view that the style utilizes the hands more than the legs. This does not hold true for the Shaolin Kempo system. The secret to unlocking the real inner strength of Shaolin Kempo is to understand its formal name roots. As stated earlier in this book, the official name of our great art is Shaolin Kempo Karate. We tend to express it more quickly as Shaolin Kempo or some even just say Kempo. As the authors we have chosen the term Shaolin Kempo because this is the term that is most widely used. However, the official name of Shaolin Kempo Karate is the best and most true way to represent the name of our style and it holds the key to higher levels of understanding.

The Shaolin part of the name represents the Chinese internal, circular aspects of our art. The Karate part of the name represents the Japanese external, linear aspects of our art. The Kempo part of the name represents the base/glue or shall we say, the fluidity that links the whole system together. Hence, the word order of the name, Shaolin Kempo Karate. The characteristic rapid, effective continuous striking; followed by defined sequences in order to produce specific results and to represent the natural and likely body movements of both defender and attacker. Shaolin Kempo predominantly maintains an upright and front facing posture during an engagement. The footwork mainly focuses on manipulation of the opponent's structure and balance, the creation of angles of attack and defense that draws the fight into close range and also, employs circular motion of the waist.

The 108 combination techniques of Shaolin Kempo develop the skills sets necessary to become an effective fighter. To be sure, all the animal techniques are informed and expressed through the Shaolin Kempo style whether the technique is from Hung gar, White crane, a family art or any other Chinese style, yet the fighting essence remains. What an accomplishment it is to seamlessly morph oneself according to the situation, all the while leading things to your desired outcome. This is the type of mastery of self that gives one access to the mastery of one's life.

WINNING STRATEGIES

Shaolin Kempo represents a particularly fierce style of fighting and Shaolin Kempo represents a style of fighting that expresses itself through defined strategies and consistent tactics.

Strategy 1. Think and grow. Always pursue knowledge.

Strategy 2. Always assume there are multiple attackers.

Strategy 3. Do not engage in order to impress, engage to return home safely.

Strategy 4. Take advantage of, and/or create folds in your attacker.

Strategy 5. Fight close in and at angles that your opponent cannot.

Strategy 6. Control begins with the initial contact.

Strategy 7. Deception lies at the heart of martial arts success.

Strategy 8. Adapt, adapt, adapt using principles, understanding, science and flow.

The first strategy of "think and grow" many of you have heard the saying, "Kempo is a thinking art." Arts do not think, we do.

As a strategy of Shaolin Kempo "think and grow" demands that people question, tear apart and put back together our practice and understanding of Shaolin Kempo. This means more than academic learning, it means that we need to assimilate the knowledge and have it change us. It demands a certain vitality and builds in its own checks and balances. If we are not growing, then we are not really thinking and if we are not thinking, then we are not really growing. It is the Yin Yang concept once again!

The second strategy, assuming there are multiple attackers, hones the idea that there is no such thing as a fair fight in the real world. Visualizing multiple attackers will always make one check one's environment and work on 'stacking' their attackers when they are attacking in multiples. 'Stacking' means to set up the attackers in a line to the best of your ability so that you are only fighting one person at a time. The second strategy also seeks to make us conscious of any possible exit. Always be aware of your exit! This strategy should profoundly affect one's practice on many levels.

The third strategy of "engage to return home safely", not to impress, essentially speaks to the utilization of focused exertion to end a confrontation. Your only goal is to return home safely! This requires an internal focus in one's training (in class and in self practice) and during an engagement. A heavy emphasis on the training of maintaining spinal alignment, structural integrity and energetic coherence evolves from this strategy. Remember: IF YOU THINK YOU CAN'T, YOU WONT AND, IF YOU THINK YOU CAN YOU WILL. You must believe in yourself and you must become the move you are performing. Zanshin is a term many throw around. It is usually defined as, "Being one with the situation or experience or activity you are engaged in at that exact moment". If you are doing a front kick, become that front kick. Let that front kick be the only thing important at that moment. Put all of your being into it, physically, mentally, and spiritually!

The fourth strategy of "folding" develops much of the flavor of Shaolin Kempo tactics. An overriding tactic in Shaolin Kempo is to compromise the attacker's structural integrity. In Shaolin Kempo, we fold and twist our opponent and their limbs, attacking key points seemingly out of nowhere and often leave them planted in the ground. Folding or closing the attacker negates or at least severely limits their ability to cause damage. The natural defensive qi (energy) of the body is called wei qi (there are many different types of qi and many books that delve extensively into discussing the different types). Wei qi is profoundly disturbed, disrupted or scattered when an attacker's structural alignment is folded. Striking someone with their wei qi disrupted in this manner pays off big in a physical confrontation. Simply stated, you will hurt them much easier and much more profoundly.

The fifth strategy of Shaolin Kempo is "in-close fighting". Shaolin Kempo does have long and mid-range distance fighting techniques. However, world-wide, it is renowned as the premier "in-close" fighting art. Physical distancing and angling strategies are inherent to Shaolin Kempo. To the casual observer, these inherent characteristics can make the art of Shaolin Kempo appear to be ugly, non-technical or even awkward at times. One of Shaolin Kempo's core strengths lies in the emphasis and ability to fight close, utilizing angles of attack and defense that are not familiar to most aggressors and takes advantage of natural movements, reactions and tendencies. Most people like to fight at a medium distance, so they can wind up their strikes and deliver what they perceive as full power. However, close in is where the Shaolin Kempo magic happens. Shaolin Kempo practitioners can and do learn how to deliver power even if they were fighting in an area the size of a small changing room or a closet. This is why we used the term ugly. It's not pretty and anyone watching from a distance cannot really see what just transpired. Shaolin Kempo students are taught not to stand directly in front of their attacker. The attacker picks the time and the place and he most likely wants to pummel you with strikes quickly and unexpectedly. You must change the time by altering the distance and you must change the place by changing the angle. IT'S A SIMPLE PLAN AND SIMPLE PLANS WORK!!

Strategy six speaks volumes to Shaolin Kempo's goal in responding to an attack, "contact equals control". Always, bear in mind that physical contact does not define an attack and control is not limited to physical contact, either. Often, the idea of brute force clouds the elegance and efficacy of this concept. The first concept introduced in our system states that we welcome contact by an aggressor. Contact Is Good Kempo. Avoiding a fight remains the best Kempo we can express, however once the situation obviates disengagement, contact becomes your greatest ally. Does contact require tactile contact? The short answer is, no. The type of contact necessary is not strictly physical and neither does it represent some mystery. Contact expresses itself as much through touch as it does through anatomical seeing and the sensitivity to read and "listening" well to the attack and the attacker. Such a strategy demands that we read our opponent from the beginning with the intent to control, that all and any contact brings the attack more and more under our control. It requires a high degree of relaxation of the mind and body and a high level of awareness.

The seventh strategy of "deception" is the oldest one in the martial arts. It is documented in the book, The Art of War (Sun Tzu) and in truth in almost every military victory in history. Have your enemy look in another direction, think that something else is happening and make decisions based on erroneous "facts" and your likelihood of victory increases exponentially!!!

Strategy eight enables our system to grow intelligently. It has been stated that Kempo is the art and ability of adaptation. The best way to adapt demands rigorous testing, understanding and solid principles. The results of applying scientific thinking to our art effectively, should never result in mere quantitative additions. In the end, each true student of our Shaolin Kempo system will develop their own strategy for winning. This is natural and represents growth and mastery.

These core strategies present the practitioner with essential concepts in the journey to the mastery of our Shaolin Kempo Karate system. Practice and study without meeting the requirements of the core strategies will not allow you to understand the true meaning of Shaolin Kempo. Remember Shaolin Kempo is more than an end product of kicking and punching.

Fighting Tactics

ALWAYS ADVANCE ON THE ATTACKER... SORT OF

The Kempo strategy of fighting in-close, can develop a tactic of always advancing on the aggressor. This may lead to tactics and interpretation of techniques and forms that do not match the true understanding of our system. In fact, many have been told by high ranking kempo masters, "Never back up! Always advance!". One can also say, "Always draw them close". The tactic of advancing on your opponent continually will remain effective as long as the attacker is slower, weaker and less agile than yourself. Most often those who will attack do so with a cowards heart and therefore, will do so only when such aspects as size, strength, numbers and speed exist to their advantage.

The skill necessary for this tactic works off of three tools: Awareness, sensitivity and contact. When entering in, a sensitivity and awareness of our own areas of vulnerability, and to those of our attacker's weapons and areas of vulnerability helps to determine the "speed" of our response. An awareness of the body language and the possibilities based on an understanding of body mechanics helps determine our movement. Contact initiates control. A fundamental key aspect of contact is to bring the benefits of awareness and sensitivity away from reactiveness to a level of control where our Kempo style dictates the fight. Drawing the attacker in as a tactic, favors soft blocks, slips and evasions rather than a hard blocking style. A hard block signals to the attacker's body that it should stop or retreat. This often results in the defender reacting to the attacker and in most cases this equals a loss of control. One exception is when such hard blocks unbalances or uproots the attacker and begins a series of disruptions to their ability to regain their balance, footing and orientation.

RESPOND TO ALL ATTACKS WITH KEMPO

When attacked by a hand strike do not think to only strike back with the hands. When attacked by a kick then do not only respond with a kick. A grab or attempted tackle/takedown does not mean that we enter "jujitsu" mode. We respond with kempo: **Strike with all your weapons and locks, chokes, take downs and your mind.** This tactic gives the Shaolin Kempo practitioner a distinct advantage. We have 108 combinations and a myriad of other techniques, not to answer specific different situations, but to teach principles!

We train against punches, and grabs and various other attacks to work the principles we will use in an actual street attack. Are the combinations sound and useful techniques for self-defense? Yes, absolutely! However, a violent non consensual confrontation is messy and wild and unpredictable. Skill is necessary and pieces of those combinations and the forms and the rest of your training will come into play, and save your life. It will not look like the thing your instructor demonstrated, though. It should not look the same either. Your response will be Shaolin Kempo and not likely all the steps of combination #19. **This is how it should be! This is what the reality of criminal violence demands.**

An adversary will have a difficult time adapting to our style, since our style does not limit the way it fights. Shaolin Kempo succeeds as a result of the principle of adaptation that is the core our system. Where Bruce Lee advocated being formless, Shaolin Kempo teaches its students to be all forms. Ultimately, just different sides of the same coin, pointing to the same goal.

HOW TO WIN A FIGHT BY BEING A JERK

Now that we have grabbed your attention; let's re-name this section as "Thousands of years of Ju-Jitsu rolled into a single statement". The statement is, "If you want to win a fight, be a jerk!" By this we mean, anytime during a physical confrontation you get the chance to grab an adversary's head, arm, elbow, wrist/fingers, leg, knee, ankle/toes you would be wise to grab it intensely and give it a sudden jerk, with a powerful circular motion towards your center of gravity. This can create an opportunity to gain the upper hand or it can be an ending move all by itself. In the heat of the motion during an altercation, many things can and do change quite quickly. Heart rate and breathing rates change, blood pressure changes, vision & hearing alertness change, fine motor skills decline.

Knowing and being aware of the above body changes is one thing, yet taking ownership of the situation at hand and the opportunities it presents, is quite another. Many times fighters will try to get to a certain move that they have in mind, perhaps it's a new move they have worked on or a tried and true move that they have successfully used in the past. This can lead the fighter to bypass a current opportunity and shoot for their "chosen move". Case in point, an adversary lunges at you with a low kick and head strike, you in turn slip the kick/you block the head strike and catch their arm and, you fall right into a simple arm bar. What happens next? Do you stay with the arm bar and drive your adversary into the ground or do you abandon this simple move that presented itself for another move? The old cliché, "If it isn't broken, don't fix it!" works tremendously well in the fast paced world of hand to hand combat. Fighting is fighting. It does not matter if it is in the dojo, gym, backyard, an amateur bout, or a professional match (Boxing, Kickboxing, MMA, and K1). It does not matter if it is in an alley, in front of a store, in a parking lot or an open field, in an elevator, in a stairwell, in a bedroom or in a car. A fight is a fight. Someone is focused on injuring, maiming or killing you!!!

Perhaps, you think we have gone off on a tangent. We seem to have veered off from the title caption of "How to win a fight by being a jerk". The goal of any confrontation is to be able to walk away unharmed. DO NOT FIGHT TO IMPRESS YOUR OPPONENT.

FIGHT TO DEFEAT YOUR OPPONENT. Should an extremity of your opponent present itself for the taking, TAKE IT and TAKE IT DECISIVELY. You need to seize it and jerk it violently towards your center in a quick and powerful tight circle. If you do this, good things will become available to you. You will have the upper hand and quite possibly a quick end to the situation. There is a way to win a fight by being a jerk. You need to put your entire power and will into the motion. If it's worth doing, it's worth doing it right!

THE MASTER KEYS OF SHAOLIN KEMPO

A Master key can be defined as a key that will unlock all doors in a particular group. The Master Keys of Shaolin Kempo are based on rules and principles for effective self protection following the method or approach embodied in our system. A rule, such as "Rely only on techniques that you are able to perform effectively at full speed" cannot be broken. This means that

if a rule is broken you are outside the realm of effective self-protection.

Treat every combination as a mini-form in application. In this manner, your understanding, knowledge and skill will be enriched. We have discussed the principles, strategies and concepts taught in Shaolin Kempo. Now, let's take a more in-depth look at the Combinations. Each Combination is a powerful fighting technique of the Shaolin Kempo system in and of itself. Each Combination is fast, effective and devastating. **It holds true that each Combination contains within itself the core teachings and concepts of our system.** As your progress in Shaolin Kempo deepens, you will invariably begin to see how more and more Combinations are actually part of the forms that are taught at each rank level. Therefore, we can benefit from analyzing each Combination from the perspective

of the Master Keys seeking their martial essence.

The **rules** and **principles** analyzed here through the combinations are the central nervous system of fighting with Shaolin Kempo, not the combinations in and of themselves. The way to use these teachings involves elevating your perception to the level where you "see" the situation / attacker(s) according to the rules and principles trained into yourself. A level where a myriad of calculations are made in an instant and you have won before any contact is made. As you train and practice, use your mind to assimilate the rules and principles in your techniques and how they create the advantage and the win for you. In the end any combination #1 or #3 or #18 or #53 for example, will expand in application to a point where they will not be able to be contained as merely a single combination any longer. You will only see possibilities and opportunities! All of your movements and actions will breathe with the power of the Shaolin Kempo system and your own warrior spirit.

It should be noted that most Shaolin Kempo schools call the Combinations by numbers and some schools use the letters of the alphabet. Additionally, some schools use names such as, "Self-Defense Maneuver's". It does not matter how the movements are named. Remember the old adage, "A rose by any other name will still smell as sweet". We have used the most common Combination numbering system in this book to convey the core teaching concepts that need to be mastered by the serious Shaolin Kempo practitioner.

Additionally, over the last few decades many Shaolin Kempo schools have added additional, "Animal Techniques" or "Kempos" to their curriculum. These movements have been added by various instructors to illustrate specific knowledge to their students. It is important for the serious student to make sure they speak to their respective teachers and always understand the core principle or strategies of every movement that is presented in their schools.

Lastly, many Shaolin Kempo practitioners struggle with why the Combinations are taught in various number orders and not taught sequentially (1, 2, 3…). There are several theories as to why this occurs and over time there will probably be even more theories added. Below is a list of some of the current theories:

1. A reference to ancient acupuncture target point charts. This theory is hard to prove or disprove because of the multitude of various charts now in use today.
2. A reference to the order spot the Combination occurs in an official form. This theory does not hold up to scrutiny once the Forms and Combinations are analyzed together.
3. The Combination numbers are correlated by teaching principles. Such as #6 & #16 are labeled as such because both moves have an initial front kick. This is a very widely popular theory. Many students look for various mathematical correlations in the numbered Combinations and some have come up with some pretty interesting observations, however in the end, that is all they are, just observations. The Western mind just loves numbers!
4. Another theory is that the members of the Black Belt society who created them did so without a curriculum in mind. When it came time to place them in a teaching curriculum instead of changing the sequence (they were originally A-Z and later changed to 1-26) to match the knowledge according to rank.
5. A teaching tool designed to assist the student in focusing on what movements the teacher is presenting. If the Combinations were taught sequentially (1,2,3...), there would be a predisposition for the student to focus on just acquiring each number. The more numbers one has, the better one must be!! If the Combinations are presented to the student out of order, it forces the student to focus on what the teacher is presenting and not on just acquiring another move. When the moves are taught out of order, the student does not know what numbered move will be presented next.

The last theory, number #5, is the one being presented as to the most likely theory by the authors of this book. However, it is critically important to remember that it does not matter why the Combinations are ordered as such, or even if one calls them by different numbers letters or names. "A rose by any other name will still smell as sweet".

The following Combinations, #1 to #30 are being presented in a basic format. We are not attempting to teach you the Combinations. We are attempting to facilitate a higher level of understanding. We will be presenting points to enhance better body mechanics as you practice each Combination. The Master Keys for each of the Combinations are being presented in **BOLD CAPITAL LETTERING**. It is important to remember that each of the **MASTER KEYS** presented below can be and are utilized sometimes simultaneously in the Combinations. For simplicity sake, we will not be listing every **MASTER KEY** that is present in each Combination. The important thing to remember is:

The Master Keys

Do Not Break The Master Keys At Any Time In Your Training!

Make sure you understand the focus points and MASTER KEY in each Combination before moving onto new material. However, this list is more of a starting point than an end list to be achieved. Over time, you will invariably come to understand more hidden movements in each of these Combinations during your practice sessions with your classmates and teacher. Due to the various nuanced differences in the way instructors can teach Combinations #1 to #30, we will not present the whole movement written out step by step. Our list is a map to the focus points and MASTER KEYS for all Shaolin Kempo practitioners to master.

Combination # 1

Focus points: Use your cat stance/block to draw the attacker off balance. Use the hand strikes to keep attacker off-balance. Manipulate their balance before picking up your leg to perform a sweep!

Master Key:

Never attempt a sweep on an adversary who is in a superior position!

Combination # 2

Focus points: Protect your centerline and expose their centerline. Manipulate the attacker's balance by pulling their lower leg (ankle area; not the knee) simultaneously outwards and upwards.

Master Key:

When in an inferior position, one must affect the adversary's balance!

Combination # 3

Focus Points: Use your evasive maneuver and multiple strikes to gain a superior position then manipulate the attacker's balance by twisting/compressing their spine.

Master Key:

Evasiveness. Shift off the line of attack when countering

One must throw/strike their adversary INTO the ground, not merely to the ground!

Folding the adversary (compromising their structural integrity in multiple directions) creates superior advantage, control and opportunity.

Combination # 4

Focus points: Use your evasive maneuver and block to draw the attacker off balance. Use the head strike to ensure that attackers head is guided into the path of your kicking leg.

Master Key:

Where the head goes the body will follow!

Combination # 5

Focus Points: Use your evasive maneuver and strike to ensure that the attacker's centerline is exposed and your centerline is not exposed. Utilize your blocking mechanism as a strike or for an arm break.

Master Key:

A block can be a strike and a strike can be a block!

It is fast and powerful to drill straight through the center of the adversary!

Combination # 6

Focus Points: Use your longest and strongest tool (kick), to get to them before they get to you. Make them run into your kick.

Master Key:

Use your adversary's power against them!

Combination #7

Focus Points: Use your evasive maneuver to create an opening which you exploit with your kick. Make them run into your kick.

Master Key:

Use your adversary's power against themselves! (Yes, it is worth repeating!!)

Evasiveness. Shift off the line of attack when countering.

Combination # 8

Focus Points: Use your evasive maneuver and power-block to gain a superior position and then use the kicking leg to take advantage of natural body reaction.

Master Key:

Anticipate and take advantage of your adversary's natural body reaction!

Combination # 9

Focus Points: Use your evasive maneuver and power-block to gain a superior position as you utilize a jerking /twisting motion of the wrist to maximize the effectiveness of your kicks.

Master Key:

Always, jerk/twist your adversary's extremities to gain a superior position!

Combination # 10

Focus Points: Use your evasive maneuver and the head strike to enhance the takedown. Focusing in on the downward spiral movement and how this manipulates the spine. Focus on the placement on your right leg/ left arm wrap and how they both enhance the takedown.

Master Key:

Takedowns that employ multiple forces are to be utilized whenever possible!

Combination # 11

Focus Points: Utilize your evasive maneuver and multiple strikes to work yourself down the body. The leg takedown should have a pushing and pulling aspect to it. A controlled ankle leads to a controlled leg/hip, which leads to a controlled spine, which leads to a superior position.

Master Key:

Control the ankle to control the leg!

Combination # 12

Focus Points: Utilize your evasive maneuver and initial kick to gain access to the centerline. The spinning back kick reduces access to your centerline while initiating an escaping pattern.

Master Key:

Expose and exploit your adversary's centerline while guarding yours! Use knowledge of anatomy to find targets you cannot see!

Combination # 13

Focus Points: Use your evasive maneuver and multiple strikes to gain a superior position then manipulate attacker's balance by utilizing a weapon from your environment (belt).

Master Key:

Always use your environment to your advantage!

(Lighting, floor surfaces, furniture placement, walls, cars, stairs, clothing, hats, glasses, sudden noises, sports equipment, household items)

Combination # 14

Focus Points: Utilize your evasive maneuver and initial block to gain a superior position by drawing the attacker in and down, while the jump kick is designed to deliver maximum force outwards/upwards.

Master Key:

Unanticipated moves land with great results!

(Be prepared for anything and to throw anything)

Combination # 15

Focus Points: Utilize your evasive maneuver and initial block to gain a superior position by getting behind the attacker. Utilize your strikes to manipulate structural integrity.

Master Key:

Kempo heaven is to be behind/outside of your adversary! Where the head goes the body will follow!

Use your adversary's power against themselves!

Folding the adversary (compromising their structural integrity in multiple directions) creates superior advantage, control and opportunity

Evasiveness. Shift off the line of attack when countering.

Anticipate and take advantage of your adversary's natural body reaction! Use knowledge of anatomy to find targets you cannot see!

Unanticipated moves usually land with great results

Never throw/strike your adversary to the floor; one must throw/strike their adversary INTO/THROUGH the floor!

We intentional listed multiple Keys on this move to remind you that more than one Key is always present.

Combination #16

Focus Points: Utilize your check kick & simultaneous arm check to stun, while you manipulate the arm bar to effect a takedown.

Master Key:

Simultaneously manipulate your adversary's upper/lower body masses! Never throw/strike your adversary to the floor; one must throw/strike their adversary INTO/THROUGH the floor!

We hope you are beginning to see that multiple Master Keys are always present and one should not break the Master Keys that are taught by the Combinations of Shaolin Kempo.

Combination #17

Focus Points: Use your evasive maneuver and head strike to enhance the takedown. Focus in on the downward spiral movement and how this manipulates the spine. Once they are on the floor, make sure they are tilted on their side and use your knee as a brace.

Master Key:

Never let your adversary lie completely flat on their back!

Combination #18

Focus Points: Use your cat stance to draw the attacker off balance. Use your hand strike to gain a superior position. Deliver a powerful downward elbow. If you are going to lift up your elbow for a downward elbow, put 100% of your mind, body, and spirit into it.

Master Key:

Gravity should always be respected and utilized.

Downward strikes should employ 100% of your bodyweight.

How many other Keys are present in this Combination?

Combination #19

Focus Points: Utilize initial stance/block to open up a low strike. Use multiple strikes to unbalance the attacker into an inferior position. Deliver a downward strike with maximum effort and convert this downward energy into the rolling maneuver.

Master Key:

Always keep moving and keep your adversary reacting to the movements and energy you have created. If your adversary is reacting, your adversary is not acting!

Combination #20

Focus Points: Use evasive entry to angle off and block & strike simultaneously. The less time there is between your initial block & strike the better your Shaolin Kempo will be! Step through the attacker with complete commitment, while trapping the arm and manipulating the head/spine for the takedown.

Master Key:

Take advantage of angles to create structural weakness! Evasiveness. Shift off the line of attack when countering.

Combination #21

Focus Points: Use evasive maneuvering and strike their limb. Move behind to Kempo Heaven and manipulate their structural integrity with an abrupt arm- twisting motion. Focus the pulling motion to your center! Finish disrupting their balance by compromising their knee.

Master Key:

Extremity destruction (arms & legs) are effective tools!

Combination #22

Focus Points: Advance on the attacker with upward blocks to disrupt your adversary's balance. Use a strike high on the body and a leg sweep in opposing directions.

Master Key:

Simultaneous manipulations of your adversary's upper and lower body masses enhance the effectiveness of your takedowns!

Combination #23

Focus Points: Use evasive maneuver and pulling trap to unbalance. Pull the limb to gain advantageous positioning and open access to centerline targets. After strikes, manipulate the head and spine to effect the throw.

Master Key:

Only step behind an adversary for a throw after compromising their balance!

Combination #24

Focus Points: Use your stance to unbalance, and double strikes to gain access to the centerline. Make sure you are always advancing.

Master Key:

Always use your momentum to your advantage!

Combination #25

Focus Point: Use evasive cat stance & block/strike simultaneously to gain access to the centerline. Let them run into your strike. The whole opening move should occur as one move. The left side of your body is Yin and the right side is Yang.

Master Key:

Always reduce or eliminate the time between your initial block & strike to keep your adversary off-guard, off-balance, and on the defensive!

Combination #26

Focus Points: Use evasive maneuvering and strike the attacking limb. Utilize strikes of incidence; by this we mean take advantage of employing strikes while your body is moving in a circle. Open the centerline and strike with a spin, continue the spin and continue striking as you unbalance the attacker by disrupting the pillar (leg).

Master Key:

Always strike your adversary from a powerful, yet mobile base!

Combination #27

Focus Points: Use scissor trap (arm/leg) to gain entry and drive through their center with multiple strikes. Keep body contact while spinning to the outside/ behind your adversary with continuous striking. Body contact allows you to learn of the attacker's intentions, sometimes before they even know their intentions.

Master Key:

Body contact is good! Remember, feel your adversary with your whole body not just your arms and hands.

Combination #28

Focus Points: Use evasive maneuvering to gain positioning to the outside. Learn to strike from where you are and keep body contact while delivering the kicks and leg sweep.

Master Key:

Strike from where you are; the unexpected is a powerful tool!

Combination #29

Focus Points: Use evasive maneuvering/strike to position yourself behind the attacker. Strike to the front of their body in the direction of compromised balance, while moving out of the way. Utilize gravity to your advantage while the attacker is on the ground and deliver the downward strikes with full intent.

Master Key:

Strikes with the adversary against an object with no "give" have increased effect. Remember, the ground is your friend!

Combination #30

Focus Points: From the ground, quickly deliver a stun kick then scissor takedown with your body weight, not just your leg power.

Master Key:

Changing the time and place is always to your advantage!

Think of how many other Master Keys this Combination employs.

As stated in the beginning of this chapter, one of the main points to remember with the Combinations is that to break a Master Key at anytime will have consequences! Please do not forget that most of the time you will be utilizing multiple Master Keys while defending yourself. Lastly, the focus points offered were just reminders/hints to keep in mind while practicing the Combinations after they have been taught to you by your instructor. There is a significant amount of hidden moves in the Shaolin Kempo Combinations. Keep practicing, keep asking questions and keep the discussion lines open with your instructor, training partners and reality. Training is truth, so always be honest enough with yourself to recognize and work on areas that need improvement.

CONCLUSION

Shaolin Kempo is diverse, profound and electrifyingly effective when worked and practiced to its fullest extent. It takes many years to find the definition of "fullest extent", yet it is an important journey. It is not the style that makes the warrior, it is the warrior that makes the style. Shaolin Kempo Karate does not divide its fighting tactics by situation. Striking with the hands, or legs, or jujitsu's or throws or locks all flow as one expression. Many of the techniques of this system end with locks throws, chokes and breaks equally along with striking. The percussive force blends with penetrating power and musculoskeletal and neuropathic manipulation to produce a rhythm and a movement that is at once devastating, as well as allowing for a myriad of possibilities.

The self development at the heart of Shaolin Kempo makes the warrior, who in turn makes the art. The principles and strategies that are developed by mastering Shaolin Kempo are most effective in winning that inner fight. The stillness, listening, control, adapting, seeking knowledge, seeking growth, stretching the mind, pushing the body and ones understanding and finally blending everything into one is true Shaolin Kempo.

A warrior is more than a fighter. A warrior is a scholar. S/he approaches life with an open mind and a hunger to learn and grow. Through defense, life is preserved and the good is protected. Through teaching good is promoted. Through dedicated practice, the standard rises ever higher and the good is proliferated in an enriched form for the future. A warrior creates. The most important creation such a person creates is herself or himself. The teachings of Shaolin Kempo return time and time again to relax, listen and adapt. Life and growth harmonize into a truth and a way of life, a Budo. The diversity of our system and the principles underlying all of Shaolin Kempo must extend to our lives, if we intend to represent truth. Structural integrity of the Spirit, Heart, Mind and

Body represents the epitome of survival. We warriors aspire to more than mere survival. These things are the "why" of being a warrior, and Shaolin Kempo shares an excellent "how" of becoming and being a warrior.

We all need to do the work, there is no free pass!

We both have a deep and passionate love for the art of Shaolin Kempo Karate. We hope that in this work, we have let you taste your own passion, experience a touch of our passion and in some manner, helped you further along the path to mastery.

Recommended Readings

There are countless good books on the martial arts, however we highly recommend these particular books for the serious student of Shaolin Kempo Karate.

American Law and The Trained Fighter, Carl Brown
The Art of War, Sun Tzu
Awakening Healing Energy Through The Tao, Mantak Chia
The Big Bloody Book of Violence, Lawrence Kane and Kris Wilder
Bodyweight Strength Training Anatomy, Bret Contreras
The Book of Five Rings, Miyamoto Musashi
The Bubishi, Patrick McCarthy
Chun Tzu's Thirteen Treatises on T'ai Chi Ch'uan, Cheng Man Ch'ing
The Complete Iron Palm, Brian Grey
Deadly Karate Blows, Brian Adams
The Five Tibetans, Christopher S. Kilham
In Search of Kempo, James Mitose
Karate-Do Kyohan, Ginshin Funakoshi
Living The Martial Way, Morgan Forrest
Shaolin Chin Na, Yang Jwing Ming
Shaolin Five Animals, Doc-Fai Wong and Jane Hallander
Steal My Art, Stuart Alve Olson
Stretching, Bob Anderson
Tao Of Jeet Kune Do, Bruce Lee
Tao Te Ching, Lao Tzu
Ultimate Kempo: The Spirit and Technique of Kosho Ryu, Jeff Driscoll
Warrior, The Way of Warriorhood, Bohdi Sanders
Watch My Back, Geoff Thompson
The Way of Energy, Lam Kam Chuen
You Are Your Own Gym, Mark Lauren with Joshua Clark
Zen In The Martial Arts, Joe Hyman

Appendix 1: From White Belt to Black Belt

Shaolin Kempo
Karate

White Belt Requirements

SALUTATIONS:	Front Position, Right foot out at elbows
STANCES:	Pine Tree, Flamingo, Horse, Half Moon, Fighting Stance
BLOCKING SYSTEMS:	8 Point Blocking
HAND STRIKES:	Front Two-Knuckle, Reverse Hammer, Back Two Knuckle, Side Hammer
KICKS:	Front Ball, Side Blade, Upward Knee, Front Instep, Side Thrust
FALLS:	Back, Front, Side and Wall Slap Outs (all to a fighting stance)
ROLLS:	Forward, Backward, Left and Right Shoulder to an On Guard Stance, Log Roll to a Ground Fighting Stance
KEMPOS:	a) Low/High b) Heavy Hammer
COMBINATIONS:	#6, #7
FORMS:	1 Pinan
JIU JITSUS:	Wrist Grabs
SPARRING:	High-Low Combinations, Introduction to fighting stances
NO-MIND (Mushin):	Blocking
AWARENESS:	Blocking Drills (minimum of 25 Swings)
INTERNAL:	Diaphragmatic Breathing (Sitting, Kneeling, Standing)
READING:	Stretching by Bob Anderson

Shaolin Kempo Karate

Yellow Belt Requirements

BLOCKING SYSTEMS:	8 Point w/Closed Hand Counters, Cross Body Palm Block
HAND STRIKES:	Thrust, Corkscrew, Palm Heel, Upward Circular Hammer, Roundhouse Elbow, Downward Elbow, Rising Sun Fist, Uppercut, Side Hammer, Back fist, Chop
KICKS:	Back Kick, Rising Heel Kick
ROLLS:	Walking Rolls
TAKEDOWNS:	Shoulder Twist, Arm Sweep Leg
KEMPOS:	a) Dropping Elbow b) Swinging Hammer
COMBINATIONS:	#2, #3
FORMS:	2 Pinan
JIU JITSUS:	Back Grabs
SPARRING:	Low / High Combinations
GRAPPLING:	Push / Pull Kneeling (on 2 Knees)
NO-MIND (Mushin):	Block with One Counter Strike
AWARENESS:	Moving Bag Drills (1-5 Count)
INTERNAL:	3 Step Breathing
READING:	Living The Martial Way by Morgan Forrest

Shaolin Kempo Karate

Orange Belt Requirements

STANCES:	Cat Stance
BLOCKING SYSTEMS:	8 Point w/Open Hand Counters, Crossing Fist (upward, downward), Dropping Palm, 2 Handed Blocks
HAND STRIKES:	Spear Hand (heaven & earth), Chicken Wrists, Cross Chop, Cross Tiger Rake
KICKS:	Roundhouse (ball & instep), Stomp Kick (heel & sole)
ROLLS:	Running Forward roll to an On Guard Stance
TAKEDOWNS:	Backward Grabbing Pull
KEMPOS:	a) Double Striker b) Driving Chops
COMBINATIONS:	#4, #5
FORMS:	1 KATA
JIU JITSUS:	Front Grabs
SPARRING:	Lateral & Diagonal Combinations
GRAPPLING:	Push / Pull (on 1 knee)
NO-MIND (Mushin):	Block with two counters
AWARENESS:	Crane Balance Drill, Defend against thrown objects
INTERNAL:	3 Step Breathing with Tension Release
READING:	Zen In The Martial Arts by Joe Hyams

Shaolin Kempo Karate

Purple Belt Requirements

BLOCKING SYSTEMS:	8 Point w/Open Hand Blocks/Counters
HAND STRIKES:	Back Hand, Circular Palm, Ridge Hand, Hook Punch
KICKS:	Spinning Kick (back & side)
ROLLS:	Dive roll to On Guard Stance
TAKEDOWNS:	Frontal Grabbing (Pull)
KEMPOS:	a) 7 Striker b) Spinning Dragon
COMBINATIONS:	#8, #18
FORMS:	2 KATA
JIU JITSUS:	Side locks
SPARRING:	Spin Techniques, Ducking
GRAPPLING:	Freestyle Kneeling: Subduing the Opposition
NO-MIND (Mushin):	Block with 3 Counters (including 1 Kick)
AWARENESS:	Point Sparring (tournament style)
INTERNAL:	Visual Imagery
READING:	The Complete Iron Palm by Brian Gray

Shaolin Kempo Karate

Blue Belt Requirements

STANCES:	Crane Stance, Closed Kneel Stance
BLOCKING SYSTEMS:	8 Point w/Twisting (block & strike)
HAND STRIKES:	U-Punch, Tiger Rakes
KICKS:	Crescent Kick, Stepping Stool Kick
TAKEDOWNS:	Tiger Stomp Takedown, Crane Throw
KEMPOS:	a) Flying Dragon b) Tiger Raker
COMBINATIONS:	#9, #12
FORMS:	Stature of the Crane
JIU JITSUS:	Headlocks
SPARRING:	Ground Fighting, Timing & Rhythm
GRAPPLING:	Basic Skill on Back (reversals & escapes)
NO-MIND (Mushin):	Vulnerable Positions: Standing
AWARENESS:	Flag Sparring (single or multiple)
INTERNAL:	Meditation with a Mantra
READING:	Deadly Karate Blows by Brian Adams

Shaolin Kempo Karate

Blue / Green Stripe Requirements

BLOCKING SYSTEM:	8 Point w/ Any Counter (kicks, punches, pokes) Monkey Block, Wing Block
HAND STRIKES:	Spinning Back fist, Tiger Palm to Groin, Tiger Mouth, Snow Leopard Strike
KICKS:	Axe Kick (reverse and forward)
TAKEDOWNS:	Major Reap, Head Twisting
KEMPOS:	a) Snow Leopard b) Flying Knees
COMBINATIONS:	#1, #10
FORMS:	3 Pinan
JIU JITSUS:	Shoulder Grabs
SPARRING:	Advanced Spinning and Jumping Techniques
GRAPPLING:	Basic skills lying on stomach (reversals & escapes)
NO-MIND (Mushin):	Vulnerable Positions: Kneeling and sitting
AWARENESS:	Takedown Drill
INTERNAL:	Meditation (flowing river)
SPEED:	3 Strikes with variety (in 1 second)
CLUBS:	Poking Club Defense
KNIVES:	Downward Defense
BOARD BREAKING:	3 Single boards, multiple striking
READING:	American Law and the Trained Fighter By Carl Brown

Shaolin Kempo Karate

Green Belt Requirements

STANCES:	Cross Stance
BLOCKING SYSTEMS:	10 Point Blocking System, Circling Tiger Bocks, Black Tiger Block, Basic Eagle Block
HAND STRIKES:	Iron Thumb, X-Strike to Throat
KICKS:	Hook Kick (heel & sole)
TAKEDOWNS:	Leg Scissoring Takedown, Tiger Roll Takedown
KEMPOS:	a) Smashing Tiger b) Tiger Kicks The Sand c) Black Tiger
COMBINATIONS:	#17, #19, #24
FORMS:	4 Pinan
JIU JITSUS:	No-Mind Front Grabs w/ Motion
SPARRING:	Initiating upper body takedown
GRAPPLING:	Freestyle Standing
NO-MIND (Mushin):	Counter with 2-3 strikes and a takedown
AWARENESS:	Boa (Snake) Seizing Drill
INTERNAL:	Stationary Chi Kung Exercises
SPEED:	3 Strikes with 1 spinning hand strike included (1 second)
CLUBS:	Club Attacks while being held with one hand
GUNS:	Frontal (close range)
KNIVES:	Slashing
STAFF:	Jo Staff Exercises
BOARD BREAKING:	Single Board with Spinning Hand Strike
READING:	In Search of Kempo By James Mitose

Shaolin Kempo Karate

Green/Stripe Requirements

STANCES:	Bow Stance (forward & reverse)
BLOCKING SYSTEMS:	Trapping Blocks
HAND STRIKES:	Leopard Paw, Trigger Finger
KICKS:	Spinning Hook Kick, Heel Kick (dropping & rising)
TAKEDOWNS:	Arm Bar Takedown, Ankle Manipulations, Leopard Tackle
KEMPOS:	a) Leopard Rolls through High Grass b) Leopard Tackles Prey c) Leopard climbs down the Tree
COMBINATIONS:	#11, #16, #21
FORMS:	5 Pinan
JIU JITSUS:	No-Mind Back Grabs w/Motion
SPARRING:	Initiating lower body takedowns
GRAPPLING:	Advanced Lockups (arms, legs, strangle holds)
NO-MIND (Mushin):	Scenario (i.e., elevators, chairs, car, hallway, etc.)
AWARENESS:	Sticky Hands Drill
SPEED:	3 Strikes with 1 Spin Included (in 1 second)
CLUBS:	Club Attacks while being restrained by Club
GUNS:	Back (close range)
KNIVES:	Poking
STAFF:	Jo Form & Application
BOARD BREAKING:	Single Board with Spinning Kick
READING:	Tao Te Ching - A New English Version By Stephen Mitchell

Shaolin Kempo Karate

Brown Belt 3rd Requirements

BLOCKING SYSTEMS:	4 Point Blocking, Basic Scissor Block
HAND STRIKES:	Crane's Wing, Immortal Man
KICKS:	Jumping Front Ball Kick
TAKEDOWNS:	Sweeping & Pulling w/Legs (scoop kicks) Hip Tosses (forward & back)
KEMPOS:	a) Crane's Wings b) Crane Takes Flight c) Hopping Crane
COMBINATIONS:	#20, #22, #23
FORMS:	3 KATA
JIU JITSUS:	Ankles & Knee Grabs
SPARRING:	Kempo Sparring; w/Striking Focus
GRAPPLING:	Kempo Sparring; w/Randori Focus
NO-MIND (Mushin):	Household Weapons, Sports Equipment Weapons
AWARENESS:	Sticky Legs Drill
INTERNAL:	Moving Chi Kung exercises
SPEED:	4 strikes with 1 spin included (in 1 second)
CLUBS:	No-Mind with Role Playing
GUNS:	Distance Techniques
KNIVES:	Front Grabs with Knife
STAFF:	Bo Staff Set /Exercises
BOARD BREAKING:	3 single boards, multiple strikes spinning
READING:	Chi Kung By Yang Jwing Ming

Shaolin Kempo
Karate

Brown Belt 2nd Requirements

BLOCKING SYSTEMS:	Upholding Block
HAND STRIKES:	Snake Bite, Buddha Palm
KICKS:	Snake Kicks (upward & Jabbing)
TAKEDOWNS:	Removing The Pillar w/Sweeping leg motion
KEMPO TECHNIQUES:	a) Snake Coils around Tree Branch b) Snake darts out Tongue c) Snake Shoots Venom
COMBINATIONS:	#13, #25, #28
FORMS:	4 KATA
JIU JITSUS:	Escape (Strategic & Technical Grabs)
SPARRING:	Blind folded
GRAPPLING (Randori):	Blind folded
NO-MIND (Mushin):	Lying Down Positions
AWARENESS:	Octagon
SPEED:	4 Strikes w/Spin & 1 kick included (in 1 second)
CLUBS:	Attacker with 2 Clubs
GUNS:	With Role Playing
KNIVES:	Back Grabs with Knife
STAFF:	Bo Staff Form #1
BOARD BREAKING:	2 boards, knees/kicks
READING:	Fountain of Youth By *Peter Kelder*

Shaolin Kempo Karate

Brown Belt 1st Requirements

BLOCKING SYSTEMS:	Dropping Elbow, Phoenix Eye, Iron Wall, Dragon hand
HAND STRIKES:	Dragon Punches
KICKS:	Smash Kick, Scissors Kick, Flying Side Kick Dragon Kicks
TAKEDOWNS:	Knocking Down Both Pillars
KEMPOS:	a) Dragon Rides the Wind b) Double Dragon c) Dragon Whips Tail
COMBINATIONS:	#14, #15, #26
FORMS:	5 KATA, 2 Person Fist Set (Optional)
JIU JITSUS:	2 Person
SPARRING:	With Multiple Partners
GRAPPLING:	2 Person
NO-MIND (Mushin):	2 Person
AWARENESS:	Dragon Circle
INTERNAL:	5 Tibetan Rites
SPEED:	4 Strikes w/Spin & 2 kicks included (in 1 second)
CLUBS:	No-Mind Role Playing **GUNS:** No-Mind Role Playing **KNIVES:** Attacker with 2 knives **STAFF:** Bo Staff Application **BOARD**
BREAKING:	2 boards, elbow & hands
READING:	Tao of Jeet Kung Do By *Bruce Lee*

Shaolin Kempo Karate

Black Belt 1st Degree Requirements

BLOCKING SYSTEMS:	Falling Leaf, First Half of Plum Tree
STANCES:	Open Kneel Stance
HAND STRIKES:	Hansuki Fist, Torque Punch, Shaolin Long Fist (plus complete exploration of spinning techniques)
KICKS:	Double jumping front ball, Tiger smashes (plus complete exploration of spinning techniques)
KEMPOS:	Waving hand in clouds, Loose hands, Snake poke, Revolving Tiger
COMBINATIONS:	#27, #29, #30, #40
FORMS:	#6 Kata, Hansuki (Tiger Form), Sai
SPARRING:	In Depth exploration of all Beginning concepts (White, Yellow, Orange)
SPEED:	Six Strikes in one second (w/spin and with kick)
INTERNAL:	Small Circulation Theory (initial)
BOARD BREAKING:	Three board with each limb (no spacing) plus one specialty break.
READINGS:	1- Shaolin Chi Na by: Dr. Yang Jwing Ming 2-Book of Five Rings by: Miyamoto Musashi

Appendix 2: Sample Questions For Grading

1. Please name five famous masters in the Shaolin Kempo Kempo lineage.

2. Please give a brief description of each of the following elements of Shaolin
    Kempo Karate:

    A- Shaolin
    B- Karate
    C- Kempo

3. How many pounds of force does it take to break an adult knee joint when striking the knee from the side?

    A- 15 lbs
    B- 30 lbs
    C- 60 lbs
    D- 120 lbs

4. In our system, at what rank are you considered a Master of the martial arts?

5. What major change has taken place in karate and kempo elements of our art?
    And why?

6. What does the word kata mean?

7. What does the word Shaolin mean?

8. What does the word kempo mean? What is its importance?

9. What does the word jo mean?

10. What does the word sensei mean? What does the word sifu mean?

11. What does the word dojo mean?

12. What does the word mushin mean?

13. What does the word qi/chi/ki mean? What is its importance in martial arts training and for general health?

14. What is the yin-yang theory all about? Tell which is which and give a brief description of their characteristics?

15. What is dotting?

16. How many official combinations are there in our system? Famous Sayings from Kempo Arts

17. The system should be your_____, Not your_____.

18. Martial arts area_____, Not a_____.

19. Fight to_____ your opponent, Not to_____.

20. What is any martial artist's most powerful tool?

21. Small steps and shuffles, forward, backward and laterally are essential in fighting. What training tool has been created to help us with this?

    A- Kata
    B- Pinans
    C- Combinations
    D- Half mooning drills

22. At what rank are you no longer considered a guest, but a martial artist?

23. Please list and briefly describe the five rules of the school.

24. Approximately what year was the first Shaolin temple built?

25. Who was Bodhidharma (Damo) and what was his significance?

26. True or False: Shaolin Ch'uan Fa is another name for Shaolin Temple Boxing.

27. What three philosophical leaders have influenced most martial arts systems?

28. Why did the Okinawa people develop open-handed fighting techniques and what is the current name of this type of fighting?

29. What group or groups of people were known to be masterful in the art of grappling?

    A-Tibetans
    B-Chinese
    C-Mongolians
    D-Japanese
    E-Hawaiians
    F-Koreans

30. Why is meditation an important part of your martial arts training?

31. Why is a straight spine essential to proper meditation?

32. Complete the phrase: Where the goes, the _____ follows.

33. What is Tao?

34. Who brought Kempo from Japan to Hawaii?

35. True or False: William Chow was a prominent master who learned from Walter Godin.

36. True or false: Nick Cerio was Ed Parker's teacher.

37. How many generations was the Kosho family art cultivated before being brought west?

38. What are the three branches that adorn the Kosho family crest?

39. What are they symbolic of?

40. What are the "praying hands" in the Kosho family Crest symbolic of?

41. What are the Hands in "front" position in the Kosho crest symbolic of?

42. What are the "hands in the form of a triangle" in the Kosho crest symbolic of?

43. Forms help to develop:

    A-Endurance, Training & Strength
    B-Stances and balance
    C-Breathing and concentration
    D-All of the above
    E-None of the above

44. True or false: Shaolin monks developed forms as a means to enhance meditation by disciplining the body.

45. When practicing forms, what position do you keep your hands in when you are not using them and why?

46. What animal is represented in #21 combination?

47. What animal is represented in #17 combination?

48. What animal is represented in #12 combination?

49. What function does the liver perform in the body? Where is it located?

50. What function does the medulla perform in the body? Where is it located

51. How does the diaphragmatic breathing assist the body in detoxification?

52. What is chi kung? How is its practice beneficial to the body?

53. What are the main objectives when escaping a grab?

54. How many half moon stances are there in #1 pinan?

55. How does #1 pinan differs from #2 pinan?

56. Name each stance in #5 pinan.

57. Yes or No: Are there any sweeps, takedowns or throws in #4 kata?

58. Traditionally, what was the flying sidekick in #5 kata used for?

59. What is the traditional difference between northern and southern kung fu?

60. The sweep in #1 combination is called

    A- A tiger takedown
    B- An axe kick sweep

C- A half-scissor takedown
D- A major reap sweep

61. How do the 8-point and 10-point blocking systems differ?

62. What is the medical name for the collar bone?

63. The medical name for the knee cap is the

A- Femur
B- Tibia
C- Patella
D- Atlas

64. When delivering a crane's wing strike, are you using the radius or ulna bone?

65. Please state the reasons why we wear a mouthguard?

66. What did the Okinawa people use to defend themselves when it became illegal to own a sword?

67. What is the difference between a major reap sweep and a minor reap sweep?

68. In #11 combination, what is the goal of the flip?

69. In Shaolin Kempo Karate, at what rank are you considered a sensei?

70. The punch at the end of #3 combination theoretically happens

a) after the takedown
b) before the takedown
c) during the takedown
d) is the takedown

Workout Routine #1

50	Jumping Jacks
1 min.	Running in Place
25	Calf Raises with forearm squeezes
25	Deep Knee Bends with Palm and Chicken Wrist Blocks
15	Squat Thrusts
25	Two Knuckle Push Ups
3	30 second Leg Holds (Together, Split, Together) 90 seconds
25 sets	Kick Extensions with Elbows Moving
1 min.	Wall Squat (knees at 90 degree angle, no hand bracing

Workout Routine #2

75	Alternative Jumping Jacks
1 Min.	Jump Rope
30	Deep Knee Bends
10	Rabbit Hops (leap higher & higher, land quietly)
2 Min.	Wall Squat (Keep your back on the wall, learn to relax)
25	Two Knuckle Push Ups (Focus on the first two knuckles)
10	Diamond push ups
30 sec.	Plank position (Keep head, back and legs in line)
10	Jack Knives
50	Leg Lifts (Keep your lower back firmly against the floor)
15	Side Sit Ups (Both sides)
50	Sit Ups (Hands on guard; don't pull on neck with them)

Workout Routine #3

100	Jumping Jacks (half Alternatives)
25	Squat Thrusts (Split Position)
35	Two Knuckle Push Ups
15	Diamond push ups
1 Min.	Plank in Diamond Position
30	Calf Raises in a Horse Stance
40	Deep Knee Bends
100 feet	Duck Walking
3 Min.	Wall Squat
2 Min.	Jumping Rope

Workout Routine #4

200	Jumping Jacks (Variety)
75	Push Ups (Variety)
30 sec.	Low Leg Lift Holds (6-8 inches)
60	Leg Lifts (all 3 ways)
30 sec.	Low Leg Lifts Holds In/Out (6-8 inches)
25	Abdominal Crunches
15	One Leg Squat Thrusts (each Leg)
60	Deep Knee Bends
60	Calf Raises
4 Min.	Wall Squat

Professor do you have any comments you want to add?

CPSIA information can be obtained
at www.ICGtesting.com
Printed in the USA
BVHW030215151119
563949BV00001B/42/P